THE KIDS WHO CRIED WOLF

Copyright © 2019 by OASM Media, Inc. All rights reserved, including the right to reproduce this book, or portions thereof, in any form. No part of this text may be reproduced, transmitted, downloaded, decompiled, reverse engineered, or stored in or introduced into any information storage and retrieval system, in any form or by any means, whether electronic or mechanical without the express written permission of the author except where permitted by law. The scanning, uploading, and distribution of this book via the Internet or via any other means without the permission of the author and publisher is illegal and punishable by law. Please purchase only authorized editions and do not participate in or encourage electronic piracy of copyrighted materials.

The publisher does not have any control over and does not assume any responsibility for third-party websites or their content.

ISBN: 9781513653952 (Hardcover)

ISBN: 9781513653938 (paperback)

ISBN: 9781513653945 (eBook)

Library of Congress Control Number: 2019948492

Table of Contents

Chapter 1: Maryville Academy	7
Chapter 2: Geraldine Muhammad	18
Chapter 3: The Village	26
Chapter 4: Lil Larry	50
Chapter 5: Premonition	55
Chapter 6: Angelo Roberts	62
Chapter 7: Craig Davis	69
Chapter 8: Our Humanity	83
Chapter 9: Conquering Fear	90
Chapter 10: Getting into Trouble	102
Chapter 11: On the Run	113
Chapter 12: Conspiracy Begins	122
Chapter 13: "Hello is this Mrs. Roscetti?"	132
Chapter 14: The Wolves Meet Calvin	138
Chapter 15: The Blueprint for Framing Us	144
Chapter 16: I Dare Them to Sue	152
Chapter 17: I Warned them About the Confessions	164
Chapter 18: Six False Details from the Conspirators	175
Chapter 19: Guess What?	188
Chapter 20: Truth Destroys Fiction	197
Chapter 21: The Smoking Gun	209
Chapter 22: Aiding and Abetting the Conspiracy	221
Chapter 23: The Killers Accept Their Fate	239

FORWARD

The Dream

Clank, clank, clank, clank! "Come on Omar, their ready for you." The guard said. I awoke and slowly scanned the holding cell located at 26th and California, court room 404. May 5th, 1988, it was the last day of the trial and the jury was deliberating my fate. The dream I was awakened from by the guard, was strange. In the dream I was in the holding cell waiting on the jury to return their verdict. I fell asleep. As I slept, I was awakened by someone next to me. As I slowly turned to look at the individual squatting next to me. A sense of calm and peace came over me. It was Lori. She had a soft glow of light surrounding her and she was smiling. She was wearing the clothing and the black coat described in the police reports. She looked great as if nothing had ever happened to her. Before I could say anything. She said, *"I'm sorry for what has happened to you and your friends."* She looked back at the old clock that hung on the wall outside the holding cell, then turned back around and looked at the watch she had on her wrist. She then looked at me and said. "Everything is going to be alright."

Omar's dream at 19 years old.

The Kids Who Cried Wolf

The Roscetti rape/homicide

By

Omar Ameer Salahadin Muhammad

Truth Wins!

Chapter 1

Maryville Academy

September 1986 I along with a friend named Louis ran away from Maryville Academy. I was 17 years old and so was Louis. I don't know where Louis is at the writing of this memoir, but Louis and I became good friends during my time at Maryville. Maryville Academy was a place for troubled children. When I think of Maryville it brings back fond memories. It was a beautiful place too. I remember when I first came to Maryville; I thought to myself. "This place is so different from the other shelters I had been in."

In fact, I ended up in Maryville after I had run away from a foster home. I Was staying with a woman and her husband named Mr. and Mrs. Hall. They were wonderful people; but I could not pull myself at that time away from going back to my neighborhood on the southside of Chicago. So, I ended up leaving the Hall home and I ended up at Maryville.

Louis was very good at playing basketball and I noticed that all the girls like the guys who played sports. That was another thing about Maryville that was different from other places I had been. They had a wide variety of events that the children could participate in. They really kept us busy. They gave us vouchers for clothing and fed the children well. In truth, there wasn't much that I needed now that I think about it as an adult.

I remember a girl I dated while at Maryville. Her name was Daisey. Daisey was a European girl and I never knew what circumstances brought Daisey to Maryville and I never asked. I would learn from a staff member; that some of the girls at Maryville were there because they were victims of molestation. The tragedy of this revelation was learning that some of the perpetrators, were fathers and uncles. I didn't realize until I went to Maryville that so many European children suffered from the same afflictions that afflict the African American communities. Daisey was the first European I had ever dated in my life. I remember Daisey was a serious kisser. Every time we were together, she wanted to kiss. She was a nice girl, very energetic and athletic. Had a temper too, but she was a nice person deep down. To this day I don't know why Daisey and I broke up. However, that would open the door for Colleen.

She too was a European girl. Extremely blonde with real glass blue eyes. Skinny with a soft personality, a very thoughtful girl for us to be so young. I guess whatever brought her to Maryville caused her to become the reflective person I came to know. It was with Colleen I learned the importance of listening to people closely when their telling you things. We broke up and it became very emotional for us both. Fortunately, we were able to recover and move on with our young lives. Behind Colleen I gave up dating for a while. A sad point in my life would soon turn to great joy and happiness.

About two weeks after the breakup with Colleen. I was called to my Supervisor's office her name was Barb. Barb tells me that she has some good news for me. My younger brother Rashied was at Maryville and would be staying at Maryville for a while. My heart burst with joy because I love my brothers Rashied and Vernon. We were separated off and on between family members and foster homes after our Mom passed when I was 4. Somehow Rashied and I was lucky to always be together. Vernon would be raised by his grandmother on his father's side of the family. While Rashied and I would be raised between relatives of our mother and our father's side of the family. Rashied and I had the same father and Vernon our older brother had a different father. Nevertheless, we would always see each other.

We grew up with a bond that transcended the brief separations. Separations that can sometimes destroy emotional bonds. Our big brother Vernon never missed the opportunity to be a big brother to us any time he was around. He always made it clear that we were his little brothers. I will always love him for that, always. When I entered the cottage that my little brother was in at Maryville Academy. I ran up to him and held him tight. I was so glad that we were together again. It is the type of bond between brothers that brothers understand especially when you grow up like me and my brothers did. I used to think that we were the only people that suffered trauma like ours, the loss of a mother at such young ages. I would later learn I was incorrect. My little brother wasn't so little anymore, we were the same height and I think he was a little taller.

As happy as I was to see Rashied, I can tell instantly the feeling was mutual. We finish putting up the little clothing he had and walked to the cottage I stayed in. I immediately led Rashied to my closet, and like brothers, what was mine was his. We really enjoyed the time we had together at Maryville.

I remember my little brother watching me play basketball. He thought I was off the chain, that is, a good ball player of course. I smile to myself, when I think about that moment, because he was laughing at the fact that I was doing something, he had never seen me do, and doing it good. I also thought about how far we had come, from the time of being molested ourselves, as 6 and 7-year-old children. I'm one year older than Rashied, and Vernon is three years older than me. It's ironic, when I reflect over that period in my life, living in the Henry Horner projects, on the westside of Chicago with my father's mom.

Chapter 2

Geraldine Muhammad

Mary Pearl Cosey was her name. A sweet loving woman, who had enough love to give me and my little brother, along with her own 13 children, my father being in that number. Many of my Grand-mom's children were adults, by the time we moved in with her. It was after my mom had succumbed to a heroin overdose, and a dispute between my mother's mom, and my dad's mom ensued after my mother's funeral. My mom's mother blamed my father, who was incarcerated at the time of my mom's death, accusing him of introducing my mother to heroin.

My dad has always disputed this account, and his siblings backed him. I personally never saw, any evidence of my father shooting heroin. But there was plenty of evidence that the people my mother hung out with did.

Back in the early 70s, the surviving parent had the right to choose who they wanted their children to be with, while that parent was incarcerated. My dad chose his mom. True to her character. My Dad's mom arranged it, where we could spend the summer vacation with my Mom's people, and during the school time; we would be with her. It worked out great because I got to grow up with my cousins on both sides of my huge family. The southside of Chicago was to me just as wonderful as the westside of Chicago. My mom's mother lived right off from 47th street, and my mom's sister Geraldine Muhammad, lived on 63rd street, in the 220 Project building. Most of the time when we would come to the southside of Chicago my little brother and me. We would be at our mother's big sister's house. What I remember most about my mom's sister, was she was a strict disciplinarian. Back then I use to think she was a child abuser. But today, I understand that everything she did, she did it out of love, and with the desire to push us all, in the right direction. Her method of discipline was firm; but her intention was good. A hardworking woman I remember. Sometimes two and three jobs to make sure we all ate.

It was after my Dad's mom passed that my brother and I moved in permanently with my Mom's sister. I was 9 years old then. During this time, I would learn about Islam, Elijah Muhammad and Warith Deen Muhammad. I can vaguely remember the Honorable Minister Louis Farrakhan. He was rarely spoken of by my aunt, and uncle Chaka. Today I know it was because they were followers of Elijah's son Warith. I was too young to understand the distinction between Warith and

Farrakhan, but it would become clear in the future. As a visitor, I never knew the difference between my aunt's home, and my Dad Mom's home. But after I moved in permanently, the differences were clear. My aunt didn't eat pork or beef. Mainly she cooked healthy foods, for breakfast and dinner. At my dad's mom home; we ate pork for breakfast and dinner. Some of my uncles and aunts smoked cigarettes' and drank. My mom's sister did none of that. But she did smoked pot.

Overall, my stay with my mom's sister from 9 years old to 11 years old, was great. But I would eventually run away from my aunt home, because one of my cousins, His name was Hassan, walked in and saw me and his sister, my cousin, playing house and trying to act like grown-up's sexually. Eventually, this would lead to the strict disciplinarian my aunt, because my cousin reported us. When I heard the chastisement, my girl cousin was getting, it scared the hell out of me. So, I ran away to the police station, and told police my aunt was a child abuser. I was young and didn't understand the type of trouble I exposed my aunt to. To this day, I regret not being strong enough to accept responsibility for my actions that day, but I had never been exposed to the type of spankings my aunt gave her children, when I was living with my Dad's mom. I love my mom's sister, and someday I will make it up to her for the pain that her 11-year-old nephew caused her.

This event led to me being removed from my aunt's custody and placed into the custody of my aunt

Diane. Diane is my Dad's younger sister. My dad was incarcerated at this time and requested that his sister take custody of me. It was 1980, six years from the date Lori Ann Roscetti would be found dead on the railroad tracks.

Chapter 3

The Village

I can still remember moving into the Village with my aunt. The Village was the given name to the ABLA Homes located on the westside of Chicago. A beautiful community then, overshadowed by the skyline of the city of Chicago. Actually; minutes away from the affluence of Downtown Chicago and the famous Maxwell street Jew-Town. I never knew why the place on Maxwell Street was called Jew-Town. I just remember going with my aunt Diane in my younger years to the stores that line the side streets, and getting good deals on clothing items, and all sorts of things. ABLA was a vast community of African Americans. ABLA Homes, was a Chicago Housing Authority (CHA) public housing development, that comprised four separate public housing projects on the Near-West Side of Chicago, Illinois. The name "ABLA" was an acronym for four different housing developments that together constituted one large site. The four housing developments that made up ABLA were: The Jane Addams Homes, Robert Brooks Homes (including the Robert Brooks Extension), Loomis Courts, and the Grace Abbott Homes totaling 3,596 units.

It spanned from Cabrini Street on the north to 15th Street on the south, and from Blue Island Avenue on the east to Ashland Avenue on the west. My aunt stayed in the 1510 W. 13th Street building. But there was another 1510 W. 14th Street building, this is the building Lil Larry known as Larry Ollins was from. In between these two buildings was the building 1520 W. 13th Street. Directly across from my building was 1440 W. 13th Street. At the other end of 14th street directly across from Lil Larry's building stood 1440 W. 14th Street. Directly across the big field from 1520 stood 1433 W. 13th Street. In the center of all 6 of these tall high- rise building was the big field, beautiful grass from one end to the other surrounded by the fire lane. Through the Big Field was a concrete path directly from 1433 to 1520. On Loomis stood one more 15 story building. 1410 was the name of that building. The Loomis Courts were located on Loomis (The 7 Story's). From Loomis to Racine were the Brooks Extensions (row houses), many row houses. From Racine to Blue Island stood the beautiful 16 story projects, the Grace Abbott Homes. The Jane Addams Homes were directly across the street on Roosevelt. This was what we called the

Village or the Ville. A Beautiful place when I was little. I went to Jefferson Elementary School right off Taylor Street. This was way before the New homes were built across Roosevelt on 13th Street. It used to be a huge vacant lot where the New Homes stand today. In fact, I remember each summer a carnival used to come and setup right where the new homes are now. Those were the days. People came from every part of our community to go to the carnival. Back then the community was close. You had crime then. But there was no crack, happy sticks nor heavy use of cocaine. The only thing I remember was the older adults, Chuckle-Luck, Page, Chico and a few other doo-woping to old 60 and 70 songs in the hallways and lobbies of the projects. If there were crimes I and my generation was too young to know or understand it.

I loved going to Jefferson Elementary. It was at this school I made a double twice. A double is when you skip a grade. While at Jefferson I would accomplish this feat twice. Once from the 3rd to the 5th and second from the 5th to the 7th. I guess you can say I was kind of smart. If I was, I didn't realize it because there were other children in my class that were way smarter than me.

Like my school mate Clarise. Clarise was a European girl and she was smart. She had a memory like an elephant. Mr. Cole our 7th grade teacher used to slap us across the head with Clarise abilities. This little girl could recite the entire Edgar Allan Poe poem "The Raven" by heart. Mr. Cole would say to us, "If little Clarise can do that, there is nothing you can't do." He would then thank her for the demonstration of concentration and focus and she would have her seat. Clarise was a shy and quiet personality. I remember, she was very kind and helpful as well. Clarise and I were friends.

Paul was another classmate of mine. Paul was Italian. He lived around the corner from the school in Little Italy. Paul was a character. He would tell us stories about his uncles who he said were actual mobsters. I never knew if Paul was telling the truth about this. Really it didn't matter because Paul was a good friend of mine. Paul would even come into the Village to play, and hangout with us, and we would go into Little Italy to hang out with Paul. One of my favorite restaurants on Taylor Street was call the "Patio", ran by Italians. I'm talking about some great food. All the teachers would send me and the other children, during lunch break, there to get their food. And I loved going. I loved the Italian Ice stand, that was right on the corner of Taylor

Street, right down the street from the Patio.

I remember my friend Maria. She was a Mexican girl. Maria was very pretty and smart. She was always trying to teach me Spanish. But I was so attracted to her, I couldn't learn a lick of Spanish.

Marcellus Bradford and I went to Jefferson Elementary. I met Bradford when we were in the 7th grade in Mr. Cole's class. Bradford was from my building; but I didn't know him that good. I would see him in passing but we wouldn't become associates until later during our youth. I remember when Bradford first came to the 7th grade. I knew he was going to have a problem with Mr. Cole. Mr. Cole was an African American teacher, and a reverend. He was also a strict disciplinarian. He wasn't an abusive person. But he kept this huge wooden paddle that he would chastise us with when we needed to be chastised.

When I reflect on Mr. Cole, Mr. Campbell and all the other great teachers at Jefferson. I realize how much they cared about the children. I realize now how much they tried to send us in a different path. Mr. Cole like all the other teachers was very honorable and just. I remember the time Mr. Cole called me to the front of class because he thought that I was cheating off Clarise during testing. I tried to explain to him that I wasn't cheating but that I was only talking to Clarise because I was finished. Because I had been caught by Mr. Cole for cheating in the past. He was convinced that I was lying and out came the paddle. Hand out and one slap to the hand for lying and cheating. Mr. Cole drilled into us that if a mistake was made, we should own it. So, I returned to my seat a bit hurt because I hadn't cheated nor told a lie. Clarise says to me, just ask him to test you again, because she had confirmed that we were only talking. Problem, we were not supposed to be talking during testing. Clarise never cheated on anything. So, Mr. Cole thought she was covering for me. I raised my hand and Mr. Cole acknowledged me. I said, "you told us that if we ever made a mistake we should own up to that mistake and be responsible." Mr. Cole verbally agreed that he told us that. I said, "I can prove I wasn't cheating. Test me again." It was a math test and he tested me again and I got them all right. He called me to the front of the class, apologized to me, and handed me his paddle. Mr. Cole put out his right hand and told me to swing the paddle. I swung the paddle. I thought It was over, and then he put out his left hand, and told me to swing the paddle. I'm older now and I understand what he was showing us. Adult's trusted with authority over others should be held to a higher standard. I will never forget that example. I will never forget Mr. Cole.

Bradford had long braids when he entered the classroom. It was obvious Marcellus was going to have problems, because he loved to talk about sports, particularly basketball, and he talked a lot in class. Gerald and Marcellus both loved basketball and played for our school's basketball team. Gerald and Marcellus were very good at the game. This is before the era of Michael Jordan. This was still the era of Dr. Julius Erving and Larry

Bird. Marcellus had a problem with coming to school late, and that led to a problem with Mr. Cole. One day Marcellus comes into class late and Mr. Cole goes in on him with verbal correction and constructive criticism. Marcellus got mad and told the teacher that he didn't want to hear it, and that he would leave the class, if Mr. Cole didn't shut up. It was very intense in the classroom, because none of us, had ever heard anyone speak to Mr. Cole like that. Mr. Cole calmly told Marcellus, that he would not stop speaking, and that he would give Marcellus $50, if Marcellus could get pass him and out the door. Marcellus got up and walked up to Mr. Cole and told him to move out of his way.

Mr. Cole Blocked the door with his body and told Marcellus to go back to his seat and sit down. Marcellus refused and tried to push Mr. Cole to the side. Wrong move! Mr. Cole, an obvious, older man then in his late 50s early 60s, grabbed Marcellus, swung him up against the wall and held him there. Marcellus wouldn't stop resisting. So, Mr. Cole remove the struggling resisting kid from the classroom into the hallway. After several minutes. He returned alone and resumed class as if nothing had ever happened. I never saw Marcellus Bradford in Jefferson again. He was transferred later to Moses Montefiore Special School a school for disruptive students. We were no more than 12 and 13 years old then.

My aunt Diane was also strict and didn't play around with me. She had one daughter. My little cousin name Veronica. She was around 6 when I moved in with her and her mom, who would become like a mom to me. I liked living with my aunt Diane because she lived on the westside and it wasn't hard for me to get to the Henry Horner Homes where my Dad's mom used to live and where our other relatives still stayed. I would travel back and forth from the Village, the Henry Horner Homes and the southside of Chicago each weekend visiting family on all these sides of the city. Later in life this would benefit me, especially during the years of the wrongful imprisonment.

Anthony Mallet who would later in life become my friend, was the neighborhood bully at the Robert Brooks Homes, when I first moved there. All the kids in 1510 W. 13th Street feared Anthony. I never like bullies. I can still remember how I used to get chased, by all the children when I first moved into 1510. I mean daily, I would get chased from school to the building. Gerald's big brother Delaney used to chase me for no other reason than I was the new kid. And the children from the building would chase me when I would have to run store errands for my aunt. One day

Baldy, K.C., Darrell, Sherone (Darrell and Sherone are Marcellus little cousins) and Andre, chased me, from the lobby of 1510 to the 7th floor right up to my apartment #707. My aunt opens the door just as I was about to stick the key into the lock. She makes all of them come into the house and discovers that she knew all their mothers. She explained to them who I was in relation to her. She said we should all be friends. From that moment in the Village I was never chased again by this group. I still had a few problems with Delaney but that would change too.

Dinky was a leader and a charmer. His brother Baldy was his loyal sidekick. Sherone and Darrell were blood brothers and younger than us all but followed Dinky. Andre and his brother Anthony were the same ages as Sherone and Darrell. They too looked up to Dinky. One day all of us are strolling through our community having fun when out of nowhere Anthony Mallet approaches us. At that time, I didn't know Anthony Mallet was the bully. But all my friends from my building knew who he was and was afraid of him. He immediately starts picking on Baldy, Dinky's little brother. Little do we know that my aunt and Dinky's mom is looking out the window at the entire incident. An incident that would solidify our friendship forever. As Anthony Mallet is picking on Baldy he looks over at me, recognizing the new face in the crowd, he comes toward me. Immediately I began swinging and punching him into complete submission, in a matter of seconds. He retreats and started heading toward the building he was from, 1440 W. 14th Street. It wouldn't be long before

Anthony Mallet gets his revenge on me. But it would take a couple of years.

Chapter 4

Lil Larry

I didn't know Lil Larry that well however we would run into each other as little kids. Lil Larry was not afraid to venture away from his building when he was little. Neither were we. And we would all play basketball at my building or play tackle football in the field next to the mental institution between Roosevelt and Taylor street on Ashland. We would also do flips off the fences that surrounded certain areas of our building. These were the years of fun and innocence. Lil Larry had family across Ashland, and in the La Claire Courts on the Southside of Chicago, bordered by Cicero Avenue. So, I didn't see Lil Larry much. Although Peter Karl in his fiction book attempts to paint Lil Larry as a horrible kid. Nothing could be further from the truth. I was living in the Village at the time Lil Larry, and the two others were arrested for the battery of the 11-year-old boy. Lil Larry was 13 and had never been in trouble before. Everyone knew Lil-Larry was hanging with the wrong kids and was implicated in the incident. He admitted hitting the other kid with the stick, urinating on his shoe and throwing matches with the other two kids. But Lil Larry said he left after that. The boy would confirm this account years later. Still because Lil Larry was present initially. He along with the other two youth were sent to juvenile detention. Lil Larry would serve 2 years in juvenile detention because he would eventually sign a false confession. In this confession, he would admit to acts he did not commit.

This false confession would play a major role, in his behavior, during his interrogation in the rape and homicide of Lori Roscetti. His two co-defendants would serve longer sentences. Lil Larry would never again be accused of anything close to that in his life, until his wrongful arrest in the Roscetti case. In fact, that case, against the 11-year-old, would be the reason Lil Larry would be chosen, as the ringleader, in the most sinister conspiracy to frame kids, in Chicago's history. The only other case that would be comparable, would be the case where the 7 and 8-year-old kids, were falsely accused of raping and killing little Ryan Harris. Just like the Central Park Five in New York. I will never forget when those babies were accused of raping and killing little Ryan Harris. I was in prison then for the Roscetti rape and homicide. I dropped to my knees, and begged God to help the two little boys. I prayed hard, and long in my cell for God to surround the boys with the protection we never had. We all know the outcome of that accusation against the 7 and 8-year-olds. I guess God heard that prayer.

Chapter 5

Premonition

Like I said earlier. There used to be a carnival that setup each summer at Roosevelt and 13th Street. I loved going to the carnival. Me and the other children in the neighborhood would have a ball.

One day after leaving the carnival and making it back to my building. Like all the other kids, I went home to get ready for the next day. But this would be the night I would have my first weird dream. In the dream me, Kimbrough, Jose, Baldy, Quinton, Dinky, Andre and others were at the carnival and we were standing in line for cotton candy. I was the last one in the line to get to the booth for cotton candy, when the guy in the booth motioned me closer. As I got closer. He whispered to me while handing me the cotton candy. "Go home before it gets dark." I turn to look at my friends and the sky changed instantly from day to night. No one seemed to notice the change but me. I start getting nervous because my curfew is 7:00 pm on school days and 8:00 pm on weekends. And my aunt Diane did not play about violating the curfew rule. So, I told the other kids I had to go. As I got to Roosevelt and Laflin to cross over I saw Joseph Jackson. While crossing over to the other side. I looked at Joe who's back was turned to me. When I reached the other side, Joe turns around and says. "What's up Omar?" I returned the greeting. "Hey Joe." Our eyes met and I could see the that the part of the eyes that give vision were gone. Joe's eyes were pure white. No black or brown circles. Nothing! I keep walking up Laflin street toward my building. But I must past a section of the Brooks Extension row houses to get to my building 1510. As I am passing thinking about what I just saw at the carnival and with Joe.

Belinda Crenshaw a classmate of mine at Jefferson calls out. "Hey Omar. You coming to school tomorrow?" When I look over to see Belinda. Her eyes were the same way.

I reply. "Yeh!" But I'm scared now, and I pick up speed and began to run toward the lobby of my building.

I get to the lobby and Chuck; Page and some more older men are in the lobby singing. I push pass Page who turns around. Looks down at me and says: "Boy, slow your ass down, you see us standing here. Your Auntie, looking for your little ass too." I fearfully look up at Page, Chuck and the others and all their eyes were the same. I fall back against the wall terrified and ran up the stairs. Seven flights of stairs to apartment #707. When I got to the door, I stuck the key into the lock turn it and let myself in. Once in I immediately locked the door and put the security chain latch on the door. I turned around and fell back on the door resting my back as I leaned upon it.

I look up my little cousin Veronica is sleeping on the couch. Right then I hear my aunt Diane's voice. "You think I'm playing with you, huh?" I turn to look down the short hallway in our apartment which leads from her room to where I'm standing. I can see her silhouette as she's coming from the back toward me, but I can't see her eyes yet. As she gets closer, she says: "Your food is on the stove. Come straight home from school tomorrow. No outside for you." Her voice awakes my little cousin who was sleeping on the couch with her head facing the back of the couch. As she turns around and opens her eyes. "Hey cuz." She says, and her eyes were the same as the others. My aunt is passing me heading to the kitchen and I can see her eyes are the same. I awake, never being able to forget this dream.

Little did I know, that in my life, I would have other powerful dreams or premonitions, about events and things to come. Today I understand that dream. We were framed so completely, so well. That a time did come in my life, where I would be able to see that friends and family, would be completely made blind by the power of a terrific lie. Everyone thought we did this crime. Only a few knew better.

Chapter 6

Angelo Roberts

1983 my Dad comes home from prison. Louis Allen Cosey is his name. He comes to my aunt Diane's home. Best day of my life. Haven't seen him since I was 9 years old. My dad has a girlfriend who lives in the Henry Horner Homes at 140 N. Woods Street. My aunt Pearline stays in the same building on the 3rd floor. My dad wants his sons now that he's home, and Diane reluctantly agree to let me go with him. My dad then proceeds to the southside of Chicago to the Bungalows to get my little brother Rashied. It was great being together with my little brother again. We moved in with our dad and his girlfriend Catherine Hawkins, her two daughters and their younger brother Willie.

It was during this time I would meet little Angelo Roberts who would become one of my dear friends. I can still recall how we met. Angelo's uncle Pierre was dating my sister in law Genise Hawkins, and he was over at our apartment visiting Genise. I was inside the apartment messing with him like I always did when he came over. On this day however, he tells me to go outside in the hallway and play with his nephew. When I opened the door to the apartment to step out into the hallway. I see this kid, a bit smaller than me, holding the leash attached to a Great Dame. That kid would be Angelo.

"Wow that's a big dog." I said. "Yeh. But he's cool he won't bite." Said Angelo. "You wanna ride him?" said Angelo. "Yeh, come on, let's ride him." I said. Downstairs we go, out the building, into the concrete field next to the Center which is overshadowed by the Lake Street EL train above our head. Angelo went first, mounting the big dog, and off he went. Then I tried. And off I went. We had a good time riding the Great Dame.

I remember my father had me enrolled into Brown Elementary School. Nice school. But again, the ritual of getting chased home started all over again. Lil Reese and a gang of other kids would chase me every day from school. So much so, that the school let me out 5 minutes before the actual time for school to end. One day

Angelo and I was walking down Lake Street heading back to my building 140 N. Woods. Angelo stayed at that time in the complex right behind Mary Thompson hospital. As we neared my building. Reese and a gang of teenagers walked up on Angelo and me. I whispered to Angelo. "Lo, that's Reese and they always chasing me. Get ready to run." Angelo replied. "You want to fight him one on one?" I said: "Yeh! But all his friends are going to jump in it." It never dawned on me until years later, that all those boys knew Angelo, and they knew he could fight. And I mean fight well! "what's up Lo?" Reese said. "Why are you hanging with that culprit?" Angelo respond: "He cool with me. You want to fight him heads up?" "Hell yeah." Reese says. Angelo turns to the crowd and says: "Look! This is head up. Anybody gets in it. I'm getting in it."

Reese and I squared off. The fight didn't last more than a minute. Reese was surprised by how well I could fight when the deck was even. I finished Reese with ease. As we walked off. Angelo said: "Man O, that was quick." We both laughed and continued to my building. Because of Angelo I was never chased from Brown Elementary School again. The last time I was close to my friend Angelo. I was in the Cook county jail fighting the case which led to my wrongful conviction. The next time I would hear about my friend would be in Statesville Correctional Center. He was killed in Chicago. I still miss him to this day. I will never forget him.

Chapter 7

Craig Davis

I would eventually return to live with my aunt Diane in the Village, because my father and I wasn't getting along. I missed my dad, but I couldn't deal with his temper. Once I was back in the Village. I had re-enroll into Jefferson. Things return to normal for me for a while.

During this time my aunt met a man name Tony. He moved in with us. I really liked Tony. He was a real nice dresser. Real clean-cut guy. It was from Tony, I got the desire to wear brush in waves, in my hair. He dressed nice too, and that rubbed off on me. My aunt didn't mess with heavy narcotics until Tony. She smoked marijuana and drank a little but that was it. However, as her relationship with Tony progress, her use of his choice of drug became her choice of drug. I don't exactly know what type of drug it was because she never used it in front of us. But I do know it was a downer. I never saw them shoot heroin nor was there any evidence on their bodies that they did it privately.

It was during this time I along with other kids would go downtown to shoplift for clothing. One Easter I shoplifted an entire suit for that day. I told my aunt that one of my friend's mom gave it to me. I don't know if she believed me or not, but I was clean that Easter. We sure had fun that day, me and Jose Bradford. We went downtown to the show. It was packed! Kids our ages everywhere! We met two girls who were from the Southside of Chicago. It turned out that they were from State Way Gardens. They had given us their phone numbers. So, a few days after Easter I call the girl I met and told her I would like to come and see her. Jose and I left the Westside and travelled to State way on the Southside. We went into her building and walked up the stairs to her floor. I remember knocking on her door and her mom answering the door. She opens the door and see two little boys standing there. She said, "Can I help you." I replied, "Yes mam, is Lisa home?" She replies, "And who are you?" and I replied, "I'm Omar, her friend from the westside." She was so surprised at how far we had come. She smiled and said come in. "Did you come all the way from the westside to see Lisa?" She said. I replied, "Yes mam." Lisa was standing in the hallway of their apartment looking at me and she was smiling. She didn't think I would come that far to see her. But I did for two reasons. One I liked Lisa and two I love travelling.

Lisa's mom was nice, but she wouldn't let us leave from the porch outside their apartment. Because of this Lisa couldn't get her friend Sabrina who Jose had met on Easter. Lisa's mom eventually called Sabrina's mom and Sabrina came to Lisa's apartment on the 7th floor. We all had a good time talking and just seeing each other again. Lisa's mom had cooked a nice meal and she offered Jose and me to eat with them. Macaroni!!! I love macaroni. I just couldn't resist. So, Jose and I readily accepted her offer. The meal was a bomb. Lisa's mom could really cook. After the meal we thanked Lisa's mom. Lisa, Sabrina, Jose and I returned to the porch. We told them we had to go and that we had a good time. Just before we left Lisa hugged me and gently kissed me on my jaw. Sabrina followed suit and kissed Jose on the jaw. Jose and I left and returned safely to the Village (ABLA).

When I reflect over my memories and the Village. I'm still amazed at how easy they come. I have so many. Jose Bradford, Marcellius Bradford's younger brother would pass after the Roscetti 4's acquittals and pardon.

Craig Davis was another childhood friend of mine. Craig stayed on the 6th floor of my building in 1510 W. 13th Street. Craig was a little different from the other kids I hung around. Craig never got into any trouble. His mom, Christine was much like my aunt, she didn't play. She was strict too. Me and Craig's connection was comic books, we were also in the same classroom at Jefferson. Craig had a sister name Susan or Suzette. I believe it was Suzette. She was the most beautiful girl I had ever seen up until that time. Her skin was perfectly black, smooth and soft. Her eyes were pure white with piercing black pupils. Her teeth were white as pearls. She had long natural black hair. When the sun struck her skin, her melanin absorbed it like food, and in return the natural oils from her body yielded a shine akin to olive oil. Simply put, she was beautiful! I had a major crush on her too.

One day after Craig and I finished drawing comic book characters. We decided we would go downstairs to the big field and practice tumbling. We had these mattresses that we had pulled from the dumpster that some family had discarded. We would use these discarded mattresses to tumble on and sharpen our tumbling skills.

After practicing on the mattresses, we would tumble directly on the grass without the mattresses. Craig was more skilled than I was, but I had greater height on my no-hand flips than Craig. When we were done. We started heading back to our building. As we were walking through the big field. We noticed Anthony Mallet and Terrell Thompson walking in the fire lane heading in the same direction we were.

He was much bigger than I last remembered. I remember when I moved back to the Village after staying with my dad for a while that Anthony had returned to Valley View juvenile detention center for a while. If I remember correctly, Jose had told me this. He also told me that Anthony was choking the other kids in the neighborhood. Practicing a sleeper hold whereby he would cut off air circulation just long enough to cause unconsciousness. As Craig and I made it to the fire lane. Terrell and Anthony are right there waiting. "What's up Omar?" Terrell said. "Hey, what's up Terrell? What's up Ant?" I replied. As soon as I responded Anthony grabs

Craig in the choke hold Jose had told me about. Craig couldn't get free.

I look into Craig's eyes and I can see the fear he is experiencing. I too was afraid. Today I realize that I was more afraid of the place that Anthony and Terrell had been, than them per se. I had never been to juvenile detention before, not during that time. I see that Craig is losing consciousness. Although I'm afraid. I know I must help Craig. I grab Anthony's arm, and I help free Craig from his grip. Terrell tried to stop me but to no avail. Once Craig is free. Anthony starts pushing me with both hands and telling me that it was one on one. Terrell agrees and is acting as if he was going to assist Anthony if he chose to attack me. Right at that moment when I felt things couldn't get any worse. My auntie Diane, who was sitting in the window watching the entire event, screamed out. "Leave him alone!!!" One thing I can say about all of us then. The children had respect for the elders. We all knew that if it got back to a parent that a child had disrespected a parent or elder. It was curtains. Both Anthony and Terrell understood this unwritten rule as well, and respectfully did exactly as they were told.

Chapter 8

Our Humanity

Children like Marcellius Bradford were the exception to the rule, and they were rare. Very rare! Luvenia Bradford was a great mom from my perspective. She gave her three sons everything they needed and sometimes whatever they asked for. Marcellius to my mind was kind of spoiled, and like most of us, lacked the father presence so badly needed during youth. Truth is, Marcellius wasn't a bad kid. Just hung around the wrong crowd like most kids at that age lacking a father figure did. Marcellius Bradford was no different. For some reason, Peter Karl, the author, of "On the Night of a Blood Moon" during his promotion of the book, did his best to dehumanize the Roscetti 4. At every turn he would refer to us as the "gang bangers" or the "4 gang bangers." Truth is, none of us were in gangs before being arrested. It was after our arrest we joined the street organization from our respective community. Larry, Marcellius and I joined the New Breed B.G.N. and followed the "Better Guided Concept for The New Breed." B.G.N. is the abbreviation for Black Gangster Nation. People outside of Chicago confuse B.G.N. for G.D. (Gangster Disciples). They're two different organizations. Both with highly organized concepts, philosophies and structures. Both originating from chaos to order and was one step away from lawful incorporation based upon the leadership's growth and development.

Because of the reality of prison life, in truth it is insane not to join an organized prison group. Due to the law of self-preservation, we were forced to. The reader must bear in mind we were nineteen, eighteen and sixteen when we were sent to these places. Real killers, real rapist, real robbers and real kidnappers. Just think over it for a minute. You're right next door to Richard Speck. John Wayne Gacy is among your prison associates. Real serial killers. Now imagine seeing these people, and others like them to varying degrees, daily. How would you process this knowing you're innocent? If it were not for the Better Guidance Concept for the New Breed, a body of positive literature. I don't think I would have been able to process the depth of the tragedy that was forced upon me. So, I thank George Davis also known as Booney Black, Reginald Lee, Jomo Kenyatta, Gam and a host of others for my present understanding. These people encouraged me to be expressive, intelligent, ambitious and righteous. This encouragement led to Marcus Garvey, Noble Drew Ali, the

Most Honorable Elijah Muhammad and their Servant the Honorable Minister Louis Farrakhan Muhammad. Surely out of darkness comes Light!

The only reason, I can see Peter Karl attempting to dehumanize four innocent teenage kids from the inner city of Chicago or the Projects. Was to appear pro-police and to boost the sale of his fiction book. In Florida, in 2019, he admits to a reporter and I will quote him. "All of the characters in the book are real except their names."

So, here he admits his true motive for the book. It was to lift the argument of the original investigators, particularly James Mercurio and James Maurer. As the reader follows my memoir of this horrible case, a tragedy to the Roscetti 4. And humbly, I say the Roscetti 4, because in truth there is two crimes involved here. The one which happened to Lori Roscetti, and the attempted murder of Larry, Calvin and me. Since Peter Karl has diligently attempted to single-handily rewrite history. I will bring the truth before the reader, to expose the character of this man, and any other, in the future, who attempt such a ridiculous foolish feat. This is the reason, why I start my memoir with my childhood, to restore what this author attempted to take away. **Our humanity**.

Chapter 9

Conquering Fear

My aunt Diane and her new boyfriend Tony are really getting serious now. He has moved in and from what I can see she's head over heels for the man. I like Tony a lot. I just hate when he is high. He's not a bad person or anything like that. It's just that I'm observant and I can see the influence it's having on my aunt. To escape what is taking place in the home. I join a dance group. It was me, Mitch and fat Tone. Mitch started the group and taught me and Tone the skills of pop locking. Funny thing was, we didn't have a name for the group. But we would go to Jew Town and dance in some of the Taverns for money. We would always take home a nice amount of money too.

Mitch was very industrious now that I think about it. He was the type of person who always knew how to earn money legitimately. Mitch taught me how to shine shoes and how to construct a shoeshine stand from wooden box crates. If we weren't dancing or shining shoes. We were with Mitch at the old card factory. Digging through the garbage for chess pieces, playing cards, exercise ropes or whatever they threw away, so that we could organize and sell. Mitch showed us how to turn nothing into something. Unfortunately, Mitch would be killed accidently by a close relative of his own family. I will always carry Mitch in my heart.

I think I excelled in school because it redirected my attention, from the pain growing up in the environment I'm from, can inflict on the mind. I remember the day Anthony Mallet would get his revenge. I was at the neighborhood swimming pool located between Loomis and 1440 W. 13th street. It was hot that day and I was leaving the pool by myself. As I exited the gate and turn right. Anthony Mallet grabbed me in his infamous headlock. He shakes me a few times which took my footing and he begins immediately applying the same pressure I seen him apply on Craig. I'm looking around for help and I see Terrell Thompson in the small crowd. No one is helping me. So, I reach out to Terrell for help and I hear him say. "Fight him man. What are you crying for?" As if on cue. Anthony flung me to the ground. I guess Anthony was finally getting his revenge. I'm exhausted from the choke hold and I stay down on one knee until I could catch my breath. Slowly I rise, a bit intimidated by what just occurred and the boldness in which he did it. "What you gonna do punk!" Anthony said. I turned to walk off and Anthony pushed me. Terrell again urged me to fight back. But I was afraid, and Anthony knew it. So, Anthony continued to press me pushing me in my face.

I begin thinking to myself, I beat this guy once, and it was easy. Well, I told myself, he's just going to have to show me what he learned in Juvenile detention. Right after that thought. I threw two straight jabs at him just like Tyrone had taught me. Both hit him perfectly. His reaction told me everything. He was shocked and the fear he had put in me jumped into him. Left, right, right, left, right all landing squarely. I had conquered the fear and Anthony. After my last punch I was grabbed from behind by Terrell. He broke up the fight. I would later learn that Terrell heard about the first fight I had with Anthony. He wanted to see if I could beat him in a fight because Anthony had beaten him. Funny thing happened behind this fight. Terrell and I became friends and so did Anthony. We would become friends and would never fight one another again. Each weekend my aunt would let me go to the southside of Chicago to visit my family in the Bongalows. This was a group of projects that was located of 41st and Cottage Grove. My aunt Geraldine stayed in 821 which was a 9-story building surrounded by three smaller 3-story buildings. My childhood friends in this area was Dennis Ware, his brother Thomas, Joseph, Famous, Jerry, Earl, Anton, Curtis, Moosey, Tracey Staples, Alex, Ray, Sweet Dee, Al Porter and a host of others unnamed but loved all the same. I was blessed to have had family on both the southside and the westside. Chicago is a vast city with a huge population.

Within the city at the time I was coming up the culture of the westside and southside was a bit different. West-siders didn't like to venture to the southside and vice-versa. But I loved the uniqueness and diversity of both sides. I especially loved being able to see my cousins Toni, Earl, Mutisa, Yusuf, Tamu, Hassan, Ayo, Yaki, Acreeba, Khalid and Malachi. I mention them all because all of them were like my brothers and sisters. My aunt Madear (Geraldine Muhammad) raised us that way. She treated us all the same. Chaka was the first real man I met. He was Acreeba, Khalid and Malachi's father and a step-in father to the rest of us. It was through him I would come to know of Islam. I would also get to see my cousin Sekou and Felicia. Sylvia Jackson, my mom's best friend, would meet my mom's big brother Omar (Melvin Saunders) and Sekou and Felicia are born. Sylvia had other children before she had my blood cousins. Their names are Petey, Lashun, Latrece and Lela. Although we were not direct blood relatives.

They were just like family. In fact, I didn't learn that we weren't blood relatives to later in life. I always saw them as my cousins and my family. And I still due to this day.

Dennis and my friendship started virtually the same way my westside friendships started. Curtis Warlow was the bully in this scenario. I met Curtis through my big cousin Yusuf. Apparently, Curtis had offended Yusuf and my cousin must have told him that he had a little cousin that could match him. Yusuf was 6-7 years older than Curtis and wouldn't think of fighting Curtis. So, when I first moved in with my aunt Geraldine. Yusuf took me outside and had me and Curtis fight. Curtis was a bit smaller than me, but he had the courage of a lion. We fought and I won. Again, little did I know that little Curtis Warlow was the boogeyman of all the other children in the neighborhood. One day I was in the playground playing with some other children and Curtis comes over. He takes the swing from another child I would come to know as Dennis. As I observed Curtis, I could see all the other children were afraid of him. So, I intervened and tried to take the swing back. True to his character, we had to fight again. Fought we did, and again I won. Curtis walked away telling me it wasn't over. Dennis, his brother Boogaloo (Thomas Ware), Ray and other would become my friends for life. I would always have a great weekend on the southside. Full of fun and good memories.

Chapter 10

Getting into Trouble

Upon my return to the westside after my weekly weekend visits. I learned my aunt Diane had been arrested for allegedly assaulting another woman in our apartment. Because she had small children, Veronica, her daughter and me. She was sentenced to do weekend time at the Cook County Correctional Center located at 26th and California. She would have to turn herself in on Friday and be released on Monday. My aunt Maxine, my aunt's sister, would watch Veronica and I, until Diane came home. After about 1 month of this, my aunt absconded and relocated to the southside of Chicago. I was saddened by this because I had to change schools. The transition wasn't hard because we moved to 47th street right down the street from Price Elementary School. This was the school I attended before running away at the age of 11 when I stayed with my aunt Geraldine. Now my aunt is literally six blocks down the street from me, a bitter but sweet move from the westside back to the southside. Now, instead of visiting the southside, I'm visiting the westside. The building we moved into, my cousin Flip (Thomas Baxter-Cosey), grandmother also lived in. Flip is my father's big brother Tommy's son, and now I'm seeing more of my cousin Flip.

During this time, I'm learning to shoplift from clothing stores way better than I did in the Village. My big cousin Flip is good at it. Pretty soon I start taking my little brother with me to Zayre's and stealing clothing for him as well. Bad move! One day my brother and I are at Zayre shoplifting, and my brother wanted this tank top t-shirt. I told him we had enough stuff and that we can come back another day and get it. But he insisted, and I reluctantly agreed to let him go back into the store to get it. When we re-entered the store, I felt uneasy. Everything was telling me to get out of there and take my brother with me. As my focus returned to the store. I noticed my little brother was no longer in sight. He was so eager to get the shirt, he left me. As I'm searching the isle to find him. I see from a distance a tall African American man holding a little kid by the arm. As I get closer to the two. I can see my brother crying. I ask the man. What did he do? The man replied, "He was stealing!" I immediately come to my brother's defense and deny the allegations. Knowing the man was right.

The man is still holding my brother's arm as he leads him to the security room. When we get to the security room the man says, "Look! I know you were stealing. I saw you put on the shirt. If you tell me what else, you have. I will let you go." Immediately my brother starts crying and then he says. "Omar, he said if we tell him what else we took, he would let us go." I am thinking, "Wait a minute. Let us go?" Right then, I knew what the outcome here was going to be. Because I still had on clothing I had stolen. Eventually, we were both arrested and taken to juvenile detention. The next morning, we were schedule for juvenile court and one of the saddest moments in my life. They called us out to appear before the judge. Susan Higgans our DCFS (Dept. of Children Family Services) caseworker was in court. Because I had been in trouble before for shoplifting the court held me for further review and released my brother. As the guards were taking me back to the bullpen. My little brother who was going in the opposite direction with our caseworker started saying. "Omar, come on where are you going?" He didn't realize that they were holding me and letting him go free. When he finally realized he started to cry. I called out to him and told him. "Don't cry. I'm alright." After I was finally released from the juvenile detention center. My caseworker had me placed with the Morgan family. The Morgan's were a nice family.

I would later discover that my little brother was not far away living with a different foster family. We would re-connect instantly. He would come and visit me, and I would visit him. I was with the Morgan's for about three months before Edward Lewis would move into the foster home. I wasn't comfortable at the Morgan's because it was so far away from the foster home where my brother was. I expressed this to my caseworker. She had me moved immediately to the Jennings foster home. I really liked it there because it was very close to where my brother was, and I could see him more. Several months later Edward Lewis moved into the Jennings home. I was glad to see him. We talked about old times and the tricks we use to play on Steve, one of Mr. Morgan's sons. Three months later Everette Pirtle moved into the Jennings home. Edward was 14 years old and Everette and I were 15 years old. This time in my life is critical. Because it's during my stay at the Jennings that I would be arrested along with Edward and an adult for sexually assaulting Everette. Detective James Mercurio and his gang of rogue cops, in orchestrating the Roscetti 4 false arrest and attempted murder. Relied on this case to choose me as a participant in the rape/homicide of Lori Roscetti. Peter Karl also uses our juvenile backgrounds to justify advancing the original crooked investigators claim that the Roscetti 4 were responsible for the death of Lori.

Here are the facts. Not only did I not touch Mr. Pirtle. The case was dropped against me and Edward Lewis. Everette stood 6 ft 1 inch. Edward and I were 5 ft 6 inches and under. When the prosecutor read off the allegation that we bent Everette over a washing machine and assaulted Everette. The Judge looked at us and looked at Everette and then stared sternly at the prosecutor. The prosecutor correctly dropped the charges. Everette Pirtle admitted to consensual sex with the adult, who was properly arrested for statutory rape.

Chapter 11

On the Run

Because of the Everette situation. I was sent to Cleveland Shelter. From there I moved in with Jackie Bonds. I stayed there for about two months. I then moved in with Edith Hall and stayed with the Hall family for several months. I ran away and my caseworker had me moved to Maryville Academy. I was 16, a few months away from 17 years old.

Maryville Academy was like I said a very nice place. I had everything I wanted. My brother was here. He had everything he wanted. The people were nice. The environment was wealthy. Didn't want for anything, but old habits die hard. Louis Johnson would ask me to go with him to a prominent clothing store to shoplift. This would be the turning point in my life that would cause my destiny to intersect with the Roscetti case. It's amazing how we're able to look back at certain choices and see the decisions that impact other events. It would be this decision that would always cause me pain when I was in prison falsely for the Roscetti case.

Louis and I went to the store to shoplift clothing and we happen to see some nice gold jewelry. We tried on some bracelets and some rings. After staring at the jewelry, we had on. We looked at one another and ran out the store with the merchandise we had been allowed to put on. We got away with the stuff and made it back to Maryville Academy. But we had taken another kid from the Academy with us. He was in another part of the store shoplifting and had no knowledge of what had happen. The store cameras showed that we all had come in together. The cops knew that the kid left behind was with us, and this knowledge led them to the Academy.

Louis and I exited our cottage room windows and was aided in our escape by a new employee in exchange for a piece of the jewelry. This employee helped us get back to Chicago from Maryville Academy which was in Des Plaines Illinois.

It was September 1986 that my feet first touched the southside of Chicago, at 821 E. 41st Street. I didn't start going on the westside, the Village, until November 1986. Lori Ann Roscetti had already been murdered before I started coming back around the old neighborhood. I remember getting off the bus at Roosevelt and Ashland and seeing postings of the rape/homicide plastered on light poles. This would be my first encounter with Lori's memory.

After exiting the bus and reading the reward poster leading to the person or persons that killed Ms. Roscetti. I headed straight for 1510 W. 13th Street to Jose Bradford's apartment on the 4th floor. To my surprise Marcellius Bradford was home from juvenile detention. He had been gone for a while and I hadn't seen him for approximately 1 year and half or more. He was much taller than I last remember and so was I. We were both about 5 ft 9 inches tall. Jose, Marcellius younger brother and a few of the other childhood friends were in the apartment visiting Marcellius. I didn't know exactly when he came home but it must have been recent. Marcellius no longer had the long braids he wore when we were younger. He wore short cropped hair cuts like me at this time. We started talking about old times and Lil Larry came up in the conversation.

He told me he was locked up with Lil Larry, Anthony Mallet, Terrell Thompson, and Gerald Charlston all friends of ours. He told me Lil Larry was out too, and that he had seen him and hung out with him a few times. He also told me that Lil Larry wasn't so little anymore and that Lil Larry was taller than us both.

Jose and I was still cool, but Marcellius and I started hanging out more, because of his hustling skills. Marcellius would introduce me to the crime of burglary. This type of property crime kept a lot of money in our pockets. Especially for me, seeing I was on run away status and wanted for a felony theft out of Des Plaines, Illinois. Because I was a ward of the state, I couldn't go to any of my relative's homes. I had to go somewhere no one would be looking for me. On the southside the police had come to my cousin's apartment and my grandma's apartment twice looking for me. My only alternative to turning myself in was the Village.

Chapter 12

Conspiracy Begins

From November 1986 to February 1987 I would be on the westside permanently but visiting the southside periodically. During this time, I was arrested once in Marcellius's apartment along with several others. This was in the early part of January 1987. I was told that I fit the description of a suspect involved in a home invasion, and that I would have to be in a line-up. Once at the police station I was asked questions about the Roscetti case. I couldn't provide the officers with any answers because I had no knowledge of the crime. I told them my name was Omar Eric Michaels, due to the warrant I had out for my arrest, and that I was on the southside at the time of that crime. I was placed in the lineup and was not identified as the individual involved in the Mary Ellen Maley case. She knew who had attacked her and cleared all of us.

We were released but Marcellius was charged with possession of stolen property. The police recovered stolen property from a few burglaries that occurred in the vicinity of Lori Roscetti's apartment building in Bradford's apartment. Bradford's apartment was where the squad would bring their stolen property to. Little did any of us know at this time, that the Roscetti case had went cold and that police were clueless, as to who had raped and murdered Lori.

In January we were hearing that police were rounding up groups of African American males, from the Village, testing them and running their background. Lil Larry would be one of these young males. I will never forget the day I was standing in the lobby of 1520 with Marcellius and I first saw Lil Larry. Just as Hoge (i.e. Marcellius Bradford) had said, Lil Larry was taller than both of us. Lil Larry seem very anxious as he spoke entering the lobby.

"Man Hoge! I don't know what's up, but the police tried to put the murder of that lady on the tracks on me. They were asking me about you." Lil Larry said. "What the fuck are they asking questions about me for. I didn't have shit to do with that." Hoge replied. "I'm just telling you man. They just let me go." Lil Larry replied. Now when I look back knowing the things I know now. I realize that this was January 25, 1987. Just two days before Hoge would be arrested by these same crooked police. I have spoken to Larry regarding that period when he was in police custody. Larry told me that the police tried to force a false confession out of him by jumping on him, beating him. Larry said, that the only thing that gave him strength to endure was remembering how signing his signature caused him to be sent to juvenile for 2 years for acts he did not commit. I can only imagine the horror Larry experienced in their custody. He said when they released him, his first thought, was to warn the hood, of what they tried to do to him.

Now it made sense when I reflect, why Larry was so anxious to tell Hoge what had happened to him in police custody. Larry understood the seriousness of what the police attempted to do to him. He was just not articulate enough to explain it to Hoge. I also realize today that James Maurer, Tom Cronin, James Mercurio and Thomas Lahm had the profile of Robert Ressler. I realize today that these men had abandon all sense of right and justice for the victim, her family and us. Closing the case was their only motive and by any means necessary. The whole world knows their version of the events leading to our arrest and convictions. Hoge allegedly confessed first naming me, Larry, Calvin and himself as the assailants. But after Calvin Ollins is arrested and signs a confession mentioning Larry Ollins (his first cousin), Marcellius Bradford and a person named Daniel. Police allegedly re-interview Bradford and tell him the fourth guy name was Daniel. Where Bradford then admits that he was with Larry, Calvin and Daniel when they all kidnap Lori and take her to the railroad tracks and eventually rob, rape and beat her to death with a piece of concrete.

I want those of you who remember how the story was conveyed to the public by James Maurer, to reflect. I want you to remember how he stood before T.V. cameras and relayed the story. I want you to reflect over every word he said Marcellius and Calvin said. I want the reader to know that the following chapters are designed to show you just how dangerous people we should trust can be. Why we must be diligent when the Creator assigns us a task and carry it out fearlessly. I know that it is my task, to tell you a story supported by facts. To prevent people like Peter Karl from ever distorting the facts of the Lori Roscetti case again. My motivation? Larry and I was watching Peter Karl on WGN news, channel 9. We were listening to him talk about how his book brought out things that was never known to the public and how he insinuates that Duane Roach and Eddie Harris are not the killers. We heard him say how he spoke to Lora Roscetti, the victim's mom. And how he talked and prayed with her and she told him she hopes the book sale millions of copies.

Chapter 13

"Hello is this Mrs. Roscetti?"

I was incensed at the thought that this man, to make some money, had manipulated a woman who had suffered so much. 90 years old! just think over that. Larry took the position that he was lying and never spoke to Lora. Because of this I went to the internet and retrieved her number. I had never spoken to Lora Roscetti before in my life. So, I was hesitant. But unlike Larry I don't like to assume anything. Was Peter Karl lying? Had he spoken to Lora? Or didn't he? My thoughts were racing. My wife, in our walk-in bathroom is running water in the jacuzzi. I look at her and tell her. "I'm going to call her and ask her." So, slowly I dial the number. The phone rang about three times. At the end of the other line. I heard a soft but strong voice. "Hello?" A woman's voice said. "Hello, is this Mrs. Roscetti?" I said. "Yes." She replied. We talk and I discover that Peter Karl had spoken the truth. I hung up the phone and I was hurt. In fact, I was crushed. I felt kind of guilty too, that I never reached out to the Roscetti's. How do you reach out to someone who had been deceived to think that you were involved in their daughter's death? Especially, their baby daughter?

Trauma goes both ways. These people destroyed us and prolonged the trauma of the Roscetti's. And here comes Peter Karl. Opening wounds, that time was healing, selfishly to make a profit. People always ask me about a book and tell me how valuable our story is. For 18 years, the thought, has never crossed my mind to seek gain from this tragedy. That's why you didn't hear from us because we were traumatized. We were hurt. There was an attempted murder on our lives by people with bad morals and character.

Every time I think of Lori. I think of my friends and me. I think of the people of Chicago. I think about her family and our families. I think about her friends. Sometimes I get upset that she didn't scream, and I cry. If only she would have screamed or fought just a little. This story would be different. I wouldn't have to write a memoir defending me and my friends. As quick as the anger come. Truth dispels it in an instant, because I know why she didn't scream. Fear! Fear affect us all differently, and I can only imagine the fear that gripped her when she ran into these two men behind her apartment building. Tears roll down my eyes now, because I know, the magnitude of what I'm attempting.

I have never written a book before. But I will be the vehicle by which the Spirit of truth dwells and tell the truth like I know it. For Lora Roscetti and her family, my wife Sabrina, Fred (son), Asia (daughter), Supreme (son), Justice (daughter), Makayla (daughter), Za' Niyah (daughter) and Za' Kiyah (daughter). My two daughters before my marriage, Keisha and La Rhonda, and my seven grandchildren.

Before I go any further, let me say to all, but to women in general. Fear is a powerful mental state, and it is known to induce three reactions.

Flight, fight or freeze. Always FIGHT!!! And if you can't fight, take flight. But never, and I say this humbly. Never freeze. Your chances of escaping a horrible situation depend upon action. Always act. It is better to die fighting than to not fight at all. We fought to come into the world. The law of nature demand that we fight to resist all forces that would impair the life the Creator gave us. This include would be killers.

Chapter 14

The Wolves Meet Calvin

This book is an ongoing fight. An intellectual battle in the supreme court of the minds of the people. We did not choose this battle. Just as we didn't choose to get framed. Sometimes, we must accept the hand the Creator deals us and honor Him by playing that hand the best way we can. Time has taught me well. That the Creator never gives us a burden too heavy to bear. So, armed with the perfect weapon of Truth. I will dispel fiction with nonfiction.

What the public never knew, was, that only Larry, Bradford and I knew each other. But neither me nor Bradford had ever met Larry's little cousin Calvin. The first time we would meet Calvin is in court. Surprise huh? It's true, we never met him until court. Calvin would bear witness to this today. Now, how does Bradford give a confession about someone he never knew? Think over that for a moment.

Calvin has no juvenile background. Never been in any trouble in his life. No arrest for anything. Never hung with Larry in the Village. No one in the Village ever heard of Calvin until we were accused of the crime. Well, how does Calvin come into the *frame*? Early in January 1987, motivated by the FBI profile. James Mercurio of Area 4 and James Ward of Public Housing North in attempting to locate Larry went to Patsy Ollins house at 1642 W. 14th Place looking for Larry. Larry wasn't there. But guess who was?

It was a 14-year-old mildly slow kid, who looked up to the police. So much so, that this kid ran up to the car, and told *wolves*, who he was, and where he lived. He told them he was Larry's cousin and that he was from the Cabrini Greene. This 14-year-old would be Calvin Ollins. Yes, I want the reader to understand the depth of official misconduct that went on in this case. Calvin would be perfect according to the FBI profile, relayed to Area 4 Detectives by Tom Cronin, a student, of the famous Profiler Robert Ressler. Who is Robert Ressler and how is he connected to the Roscetti case? From October 18, 1986 until January 27, 1987 these idiots, had no clue who committed this brutal crime. That's three months!

All they had was the O-secretor blood-type of the semen from whoever had killed the poor woman and a partial palm print. It must be clearly understood by the reader, that James Maurer, Tom Cronin, James Mercurio, Thomas Lahm and all the original investigators knew, the blood type of the Semen found in Lori Roscetti and knew that it was from the killer. Susan Sussman, the prosecutor who approved charges against us knew. Patrick O' Brien and George Velcich, the prosecutors assigned to the case by then State's Attorney Richard M. Daley knew. The only person that didn't know, was Mayor Harold Washington, the first African American Mayor of the city of Chicago. And I think we all know why. There would have been a lot of people fired and in jail for what we know really happened in the Roscetti case.

Chapter 15

The Blueprint for Framing Us

Robert Kenneth Ressler (February 21, 1937-May 5, 2013) was an FBI agent and author. He played a major role in the psychological profiling of violent criminals in the 1970s and is often credited with coining the term "serial killer." Ressler joined the FBI in 1970 and was recruited into the Behavioral Science Unit that deals with drawing up psychological profiles of violent criminals, such as rapists and serial killers, who typically select victims at random. He worked on many cases of serial homicide such as John Joubert, Jeffrey Dahmer, Richard Chase and Ted Bundy to name a few. From my research of Mr. Ressler. He was a man of impeccable character. Before joining the FBI, Mr. Ressler was a major in the army. No one has denied his level of expertise, integrity or honor. His words and opinions in this field were like gold. Mr. Ressler would pass in 2013 from Parkinson's disease at his home amongst his family.

According to Mr. Ressler in his book entitled "Whoever Fights Monsters." Tom Cronin contacted him about the Roscetti case, sending him all the documentation he needed to produce a profile. According to what I read in Robert Ressler's book on page 166. Mr. Ressler says he gave Tom Cronin an oral profile at his (Tom Cronin) home. The profile which became the blueprint for framing the Roscetti 4.

Tom Cronin was involved in the Roscetti case. Tom Cronin is the link by which James Maurer, James Mercurio and Thomas Lahm received Robert Ressler's profile of the Roscetti case. Tom Cronin was a student of Ressler and was well acquainted with

Ressler. Unfortunately, Tom Cronin stood by and watched an honorable man slandered by his corrupt buddy James Maurer on a national platform, Dateline NBC. The program was called "And Justice for All" a Dateline Special. James Maurer calls Ressler a "liar." He says, "Robert Ressler arrived in his office the morning they had these people in custody." Robert Ressler insisted that he told Tom Cronin exactly what Calvin and Bradford's confession say before they were arrested. Mr. Ressler died standing upon the fact that he gave this profile to Tom Cronin before the

Roscetti 4 were ever arrested. His book, 'Whoever Fights Monsters' is still being sold. And it is a great book.

It's strange that only the original investigators are calling an Honorable man a liar. James Maurer, James Mecurio, Thomas Lahm and Cronin all say that the Roscetti 4 are liars. They say that Duane Roach and Eddie Harris are liars. That they didn't kill Lori Roscetti. Their position is that Duane Roach and Eddie Harris did kidnap Lori in the alley behind her building, they took her and the car after stopping for food, alcohol, and drugs up to the railroad tracks at 15th and Loomis, there they both brutally raped her and then they give her back her car keys and let her go. On her way home, she was abducted again by Larry, Calvin, Marcellius and me at Loomis and Flournoy. Taken back to the exact spot the first two offenders had taken her, robbed, raped and beat to death by the Roscetti 4.

Here's the problem. God didn't allow these criminals with badges to see the future. They never could have conceived of a science call DNA. This is the only reason they would go all out-fabricating confessions, taking pictures of the teenagers before the interrogations, and conspiring with one another to make the confessions believable. Remember I said earlier that everyone knew that the blood type of the semen was O-secretor?

Did you know that these same people knew that the Roscetti 4 were all non-secretors? Unbelievable huh? It's true. Calvin and Larry are type O-nonsecretors (i.e. Lewis negatives), Bradford is type A-nonsecretor, and

I'm type B-nonsecretor. A secretor is a person that secretes their blood in bodily fluids other than blood. Like semen, saliva, sweat or vaginal fluids. A nonsecretor's blood type can only be detected in their blood.

Chapter 16

I Dare Them to Sue

Why didn't our blood type matter anymore in 1987? Just think over that for a minute. It is because we were chosen long before our arrest, by corrupt police to be the scapegoats for a crime James Maurer, Tom Cronin,

James Mercurio, Thomas Lahm, Susan Sussman, and a host of others could not solve? You may be wondering why I mention Susan Sussman, Patrick O' Brien and George Velcich, all assistant state's attorneys, under Richard M. Daley at the time. That's simple. They all became aware of the framing of the Roscetti 4 and conspired to aid and abet the crime. Yes, it was and is a crime what they did. Listen close. I dare any of these people to sue me for libel or slander. Remember, truth is an absolute defense against those type of claims. I would love to reopen this case and air out their dirty laundry in a courtroom. But for now, this media is enough. Official Misconduct is a crime in Illinois. I wonder if we can still go to the attorney registration and disciplinary commission on all the attorneys involved in this case?

How did Pamela Fish miss 20 semen stains? Out of 22 semen stains she only finds two on the vaginal swab and underwear! A conspiracy is defined as "the act of conspiring together." To do what? Achieve a desired result or a common goal. Pamela Fish was employed by the

Chicago Police Department. James Maurer and the gang needed the blood to fit people they had lied on. To make the lie credible the most critical piece of evidence was twisted by Pam Fish, a co-conspirator, to make the fabricated confessions believable to the public and future juries.

Why was it important to omit the other 20 semen stains and lie about the blood type of the two you admit you found? Just imagine you're a juror and you hear this incredible confession, but the key evidence, which all admit came from the killer, doesn't match any of the accused. Nor does any of the other 20 semen stains! What would come to your mind about the confessions which are literally handwritten by the conspirators and stenographer? Neither Calvin nor Bradford has a handwritten confession. The confessions signed by Calvin and Bradford were *literally* written word for word by the conspirators. Both Calvin and Bradford say that the confessions were already written, they just signed them.

How do we know today that the confessions are absolute fabrications of James Maurer and the gang? Because they are identical to FBI expert Robert Ressler profile, he gave to their buddy an associate Tom Cronin. Filled in with details only the real killers and *police* would know. *Every detail* in the fabricated confessions was known to Maurer and the gang. All the way down to Lori's missing car keys.

In a police report dated January 31, 1987 James Mercurio and Thomas

Lahm writes: "Bradford said he was not aware that the victim's **key**s were taken until sometimes in December when Calvin took some **key**s out of his pocket and asked, "Remember these?" These criminals go further and write: "Calvin also said that he took the victim's **key**s off her ring and put them on his. He said that he kept the **key**s for a couple of weeks, but Larry Ollins told him to throw them away. Calvin said he threw away the gym shoes that he wore on the night they killed Lori Roscetti because they were worn out."

I just want the reader of this memoir to understand the type of sick, demented and twisted people the original investigators were and are. In 2002 the new investigators are interviewing Duane Roach. Mind you, this is a video re-enactment of the crime, where he takes the investigator step by step explaining what happen to Lori on that fateful night. At the very end of the video the investigator says to Duane Roach: "When we were coming over from Racine and Roosevelt and we're driving down Loomis and you pointed out a sewer to us. Is that correct?" Duane Roach replies: "Yes. Because I still had her car keys in my pocket." Investigator: "Okay you just remembered that as we were coming by the sewer?" Duane Roach: "Yeah, I remember as we were coming by. I had her car keys in my pocket." The investigator then takes Duane Roach to where he says he threw the victim's keys down a sewer on 14th and Loomis after he left the crime scene (i.e. railroad tracks). This was totally unsolicited by the investigator. Duane Roach, in re-enacting his role in the crime, remembered what he did with her car keys after he left the victim and Eddie

Harris up on the railroad tracks. Duane Roach has also confessed that during the abduction of Lori. He was the one who took her keys and drove her vehicle which was a stick shift.

How could Bradford and Calvin, in separate interrogation rooms, mention seeing keys or having keys, Duane Roach discarded via a sewer after he left the victim and her car, along with his codefendant up on the railroad embankment/track? This detail is *critical*. Why? Go back and read what these criminals said

Bradford and Calvin said. Look at how *easy* they're doing it. Read it knowing that the real killers and the Roscetti 4 have never met. They were adults and we were teenage kids with marginal backgrounds, all but Calvin Ollins. Both confessions have Bradford and Calvin in separate rooms saying that the Roscetti 4 abducted Lori at approximately 1:00 am or so in the morning. Or so means, a little after 1:00 am. It is a known fact that Lori and Allen Radner reached her car at 1:00 am and that she dropped him off and went straight home. It is also, a known fact, that from the hospital to her apartment building takes less than 6 minutes in a vehicle. So, Lori would have made it home no later than 1:15 am. Which meant, Duane Roach and Eddie Harris abducted her around 1:15 am to 1:20 am.

How could Bradford and Calvin in separate rooms invent an *'impossible abduction'* at the same time (i.e. 1:00am or so in the morning)? Who would know other than the real killers and the *police* the actual time or approximate time of the real abduction? ***The Conspirators!***

Chapter 17

I warned Them About the Confessions

The day I walked out of prison 18 years ago. Before Duane Roach and Eddie Harris were even a thought. I warned Maurer and the gang that the two confession would be their undoing. They kept saying: **"The confessions contained details only the killers would have known. Just because the DNA exonerated them**

of the rape that doesn't mean they didn't kill her. " 30 days later Bernard Roach the blood brother of Duane Roach, turns his brother in. They get Bernard to wear a wire to entrap his brother, and they run an elaborate ruse on Eddie Harris to get him to admit his involvement. It all worked. The new investigators were thorough leaving no room for mistake. Come to find out. Just days after Lori's rape and murder. Duane Roach had admitted to his brother Bernard, that he and Eddie Harris had killed Lori and that, "she was a tough bitch to kill." According to Duane Roach.

Peter Karl in order to sell his fiction book pushes the two-abduction theory advance by disgraced detective James Mercurio.

Here's the problem with that theory. Had Peter Karl really paid attention to the video tape re-enactments of the killers and read Mercurio's other confession, a thirteen-page statement trying to save his butt, or just really combed through the two false confession. He would have realized why Phil Cline told Jodi Wilgoren of the New York Times: "We're satisfied that these two individuals are the ones who were responsible for the sexual assault and murder," "They took her to the access road, where they sexually assaulted her, and subsequently murdered her," he said. "Their stories match the physical evidence that was there back in 1986."

Phil Cline oversaw the new investigation that lead to the real killers. Truth is, the police didn't solve the case. Bernard Roach did. If it was not for Bernard Roach coming forward on his own brother. This case may have never been solved.

Maurer and the gang really did a number on the people of Chicago. Their actions were despicable. They hijacked Robert Ressler's profile. Which was accurate, except for where the abduction occurred on her way home, and how many people were involved. They created a story so believable, due to details they added. Then colored these details with a vicious scenario of four depraved youth and fed the concoction to the media.

For example. I turned myself in for questioning only after I was filmed by Rush Ewing of channel 7 eyewitness news. I went to see Bradford using the identification of a friend from the Village.

When I saw Bradford. The first thing he said was. "Man O, I didn't do this shit. I don't even know the young motherfucker they saying I did this shit with. I know L, but I aint never met his cousin man." Before I could say anything. Bradford says. "They tried to make me put you in this shit."

It was this visit that made me aware some serious stuff was going down.

Therefore, I allowed Rush Ewing to film me walking into the police station on 71st and Cottage Grove. To ensure that they wouldn't try to force me to sign something they had made up. Turning myself in to Rush Ewing was Luvenia Bradford's idea. If I was smarter, I would have walked in with a lawyer. Rush Ewing promised me that he would stay with me through the questioning, but left right after he walked me in.

I was transported to Area 4 for questioning. The gang showed me a type written statement where Bradford is allegedly implicating me in the Roscetti crime. They tell me that they know he is lying, and that I had nothing to do with it. Their telling me Bradford is not my friend and that Larry, Calvin, Bradford and a guy named Daniel committed the crime. All they need me to do is say. That I was up on the tracks attempting to break in some carts when I heard a scream. As I walked toward the scream. I see Larry, Calvin, Bradford and another guy I can't identify that well. Of course, I refused to cooperate, and they tell me to help myself or they can make me the fourth guy. I refuse to cooperate, and I'm left in a room for hours chained to a ring in the wall. After being in the room for unknown hours. Susan Sussman enters the room and I tell her. They tried to get me to lie on Hoge and the others. She looked me straight in the eyes and told me to, "Cut the bullshit and save yourself." The next thing I know. I'm being handcuff with my hands behind my back and charged with murder.

I would later learn that Mercurio said he had told me: *"that there were two hairs found on the driver's seat of the victim's auto and that there was sperm found in the victim. You and Calvin were the only ones who fucked her in the front seat. How long did Calvin fuck her?* Saunders responded, *"For only a couple of minutes."* Mercurio then said, *"Do you realize the hairs found on the front seat may be traced to you or Calvin?"* In response Saunders said, *"Yes, I realize that."*

I didn't say any of this perverted stuff. Notice how he uses the terms "fucked her" and "fuck her." These terms are in the confession they attribute to Bradford and Calvin. All of this is completely from his sick mind. Pay attention to his knowledge of the details of the crime scene. Look at how he uses the details to create another scenario to frame me. Just as they did the others. I wouldn't cooperate. So, this criminal and the gang wrote me into the hijacked profile of Robert Ressler, for two reasons. One, I came in with the news and two, they tried to get me to lie on the others. **They couldn't let me go. I knew way too much.** Time would demonstrate, I would become their worst nightmare, and they should've!

Chapter 18

Six false details from conspirators

I told these criminals that the two confessions would be their undoing. In this nonfiction/memoir, I will expose to the reader word for word, as to what Mecurio and the gang wrote. Today Maurer and the gang don't dispute that Duane Roach and Eddie Harris, the real killers, abducted Lori behind her house in the alley *at 1:00 or so in the morning*. The same alley where they found the footprints in 1986 that were like the one found on her chest. Today, there is no dispute that Lori was **never abducted at Loomis and Flournoy <u>by the Roscetti 4</u>** at 1:00 am or so in the morning as mentioned in the confessions written by James Mercurio, Susan Sussman, Youth officer Harry Drochner, and Raymon F. Peter.

How could Calvin and Bradford in separate interrogation rooms *invent* this false detail? Both confessions say Larry Ollins jumped in the passenger side of Lori's vehicle at Loomis and Flournoy. How could Bradford and Calvin *invent* this false detail in separate rooms? Both confessions say at Loomis and Flournoy, Larry Ollins unlocked the back doors. How could Bradford and Calvin in separate rooms *invent* this false detail? Both confessions say that Marcellius Bradford got into the front passenger side of Lori's car at Loomis and Flournoy. How could Bradford and Calvin in separate rooms *invent* this false detail? Both confessions say Calvin Ollins grabbed Lori around the neck and pulled her into the back seat at Loomis and Flournoy. How could Bradford and Calvin in separate rooms *invent* this false detail? All in the same order!!! **Truth wins.**

Six details that are clearly false, didn't come from these boys. It came from a single story which originated in the mind of Mecurio and his gang of co-conspirators. A story hijacked from FBI profiler Robert K. Ressler. It is clear the confessions are fabrications of the conspirators. This is and was "official misconduct," in the legal meaning of that statute. And at the highest level.

They thought they did a perfect job framing us and they did. But America is founded upon divine principles. Divine destruction or chastisement is the Creator manifesting what we do in the dark and bringing it to the light. A Republic is maintained by responsible sober-minded beings. America has a wonderful destiny. Unfortunately, people like this will not be a part of that destiny. The mind-set exposed by the Roscetti case is typical of those Europeans afflicted with a false sense of their own value. This is the only way that these **wolves** could devalue the Roscetti 4 the way they did and continue to try. As demonstrated by Peter Karl in his fiction book, "On the Night of a Blood Moon."

He calls himself an investigative reporter, and boast of attainments that are worthless, where there is lack of respect for others. He claims to have these same *facts* that I have shared herein. But for a dollar he ignored the obvious and I believe, misled Lora Roscetti. She said to me on the phone. "I think it was a good book." I thought to myself, respectfully. "A book that insinuate that there were two abductions. The first being Duane Roach and Eddie Harris and the second being the Roscetti 4, who then kills her?" Unacceptable!

The only way he could have convinced this poor woman of something so preposterous, was to omit the facts I have outlined in this book. He used the same fabricated confessions, to make the same arguments that the co-conspirators used 30 years ago, to send four innocent boys to prison. He thought that since the Roscetti Brothers were quiet, and no one has heard from us in 18 years, maybe he could twist the history, and call it fiction, and make a profit. If I had been a juror and heard these confessions, and the alleged admissions that the conspirators spun, I would have sent us to prison too. Peter Karl makes the argument and convincingly, to those who don't know the *facts* of the case. That the Roscetti 4 were involved. Well, keep reading.

One of his arguments he has made over the radio and television is that Duane Roach and Eddie Harris say that Lori was struck with the concrete in her vehicle. Nothing can be further from the truth. Eddie

Harris is apprehended first. He is setup by Bernard Roach at the police station where he admits his involvement in the crime. After Eddie realizes that Bernard set him up. He gives the first video tape re-enactment confession trying to place the blame on Duane Roach, who he obviously thinks is a part of the setup. So naturally, he is trying to save his on hide and direct all the blame onto Duane.

In Eddie's confession he admits to raping Lori on the railroad tracks in the back seat of her car. He claims that he only had vaginal intercourse with Lori. What Eddie didn't know was that the new investigators had the 22 semen stains and knew where each was found. Both Eddie and Duane had anally assaulted Lori, DNA from both men was found in her rectum. Eddie doesn't mention this assault in his confession. But does that mean he didn't commit an anal assault because he doesn't mention it? Eddie doesn't mention the size 12 footprint found on Lori's torso. Eddie wore a size 12 to 13 shoe. Which means, Eddie was the one stomping her and crushed her larynx that night. This was the same footprint found behind her apartment building in 1986. Does it mean he didn't stomp Lori crushing her ribs and her larynx because he didn't mention it? None of the Roscetti 4 wore a size 12 shoe. Eddie doesn't mention slamming Lori's head with the front passenger door either, but Duane Roach does. This act caused the lacerations to Lori's head.

Eddie says, that Duane while sitting in the driver's seat of the car was scratched in the face by Lori, who was sitting in the front passenger seat. This allegedly caused Duane to open the driver's door, reach down, grab a large chunk of concrete, and strike Lori in the face inside the car. The new investigator and I knew this couldn't have happen this way; because there was a perfect halo of Lori's blood in the front passenger's seat. This blood could not have gotten there the way Eddie described it. So, Eddie was lying. Like most killers do. Fact, they both mention in their confession the murder weapon, **the concrete!**

Chapter 19

Guess What

Duane gave two video tape confessions. One an oral confession, and the other a re-enactment of the night he and Eddie kidnapped, robbed, raped and killed Lori. In Duane's confession he admits to the abduction, robbery, and rape but he denies killing Lori.

Duane says that Eddie grabbed Lori by the hair in the front seats with her head toward the passenger door. He then pulled her head to a position where he slammed the passenger door with tremendous force on Lori's head, rendering her unconscious. This would explain the large halo pattern of blood found on the front passenger seat. Afterward, says Duane, Eddie pulled Lori from the car via the passenger door and laid her on the side of the car. This is **exactly** how crime scene photos depict Lori's body. After being removed from the car. Duane says, that Eddie Harris struck Lori in the face with the large concrete that Eddie said Duane hit her with in the car. I think we all know by now who's telling the truth. If you said Duane. You're partly correct.

Duane can't talk about the knife wounds to her torso nor the footprints because he left Eddie there just like he said he did. Eddie admit to drinking a 40 ounce of beer at the scene before the rape. He admits they had weed, and that Duane had a half-a-pint of liquor. This is the atmosphere in which Lori found herself that night. Yes, Eddie Harris had a knife that night, and there were multiple puncture wounds on Lori's torso.

There was also a laceration to Lori's neck from where Eddie was holding the knife to Lori, just like Duane described.

These details are interesting because the original investigators didn't know a knife was used although they found Eddie's knife that night. They attributed the puncture wounds to a sharp pointed wooden stick given to her by her brother for protection. In fact, this detail ends up in the false confession of Marcellius as the stick Calvin Ollins is poking and hitting

Lori with. Now that we know the conspirators fabricated the confessions with intricate details that only they and the real killers knew. We can now explain how those puncture wounds on Lori's torso got there. Eddie's knife!

Duane says he told Eddie after He slammed her head in the door and dragged her out the car, that the woman still had a pulse. Duane said to Eddie, "she still breathing." Duane said he stood up and turned around to look to see if anyone was coming.

Duane says as he was doing this, he heard "a crushing sound." When he turned around, he saw that Eddie Harris had hit Lori with the large chunk of concrete in the face.

The way Duane says Eddie slammed her head in the door and hit her with the concrete shows he was trying to kill her. The knife was used by Eddie to make sure she was dead. Eddie was poking Lori multiple times to ensure that there was no sign of life. When I watch the reenactments of Duane Roach and Eddie Harris's videos. My *instincts* tell me that Duane slammed Lori's head in the door, and he pulled her from the car and laid her on the ground. Therefore, I say Duane is partly telling the truth.

But Eddie did, crush her head in with the concrete, stomped her, fracturing her ribs, crushed her larynx and stabbed her multiple times with the knife to make sure she was dead. Whoever left the footprint killed Lori. Eddie wore a size 12 shoe. Either way, they are both liable for the actions of the other. "She was a tough bitch to kill.", says Duane two days after Lori's murder. "Me and Eddie did that." He tells his brother Bernard Roach. In these words of **truth** are the evidence that he participated in the brutal beating Lori sustained to her body. Plus, Duane had been convicted for rapes in the past. He had way more to lose if caught than Eddie. For this reason, I believe he participated in the physical assault, and the brutal beating that lead to Lori's death. Furthermore, this confession of killing Lori, is 30 years prior to his arrest and 3 months before the Roscetti 4 would be falsely accused by bundling idiots.

These comments by Duane are not made under threat, duress or coercion. Peter Karl claims that he spoke to these men and they said they didn't kill Lori. Guess what?

I spoke to Richard Speck and he told me the same thing. "I didn't kill all those nurses." He said.

Because Peter Karl has launched this book and went to radio and television stations doing what I think is defamatory. I must defend the Roscetti 4 and even Robert Ressler from those who would seek to distort history and the facts. What the Roscetti Brother's (i.e. Larry and I) found strange, was the acknowledgements Mr. Karl gave to Tom Cronin, Phil Cline, and Kathleen T. Zellner. Why would he be thanking Zellner and Cline, two people who know that we're innocent? Why would Kathy be supporting a book that would insinuate her former clients are the possible killers.

Chapter 20

Truth Destroys Fiction

What most people don't know is how Larry, Bradford and my relationship ended with Kathy (i.e. Kathleen T. Zellner). What I will say, is that we were close, especially Kathy and me. That's for another book. But back to the Roscetti case.

After the exoneration of the Roscetti 4 and the arrest of Duane Roach and Eddie Harris. Maurer and the gang shut up. No more talking. Silence could be heard from Chicago to China. Not a peep! It was looking grim for Maurer and the gang, who claimed on national television that, *"This case was solved by good-ole-fashion police work!"* In fact, Mercurio had some explaining to do. So, he was charged with writing a 13-page explanation of what he thinks happened. I will quote, word for word some of his brilliant conclusions:

"The previously convicted offenders did not talk about Roach and Harris because they did not see them at whatever place they actually assaulted the victim. These two groups never talked

about each other because they never came into contact with each other. I believe it was obvious that two separate incidents took place. Part 1 was Roach and Harris abducting the victim with the knife, having sex with her, and releasing the victim. Part 2 was the abduction, aggravated criminal sexual assault, and murder by the 2nd group while the victim was on her way home...............Neither group of arrestees said the other group was present. I believe there is only one *logical conclusion*. After Roach and Harris abducted

Lori Roscetti in back of her house they took her somewhere and sexually assaulted her. They then let her go. On her way home she was abducted by Larry Ollins, Marcellius Bradford, Calvin Ollins, Omar Saunders and possibly a person known as Daniel."

This is where Peter Karl's operating theory originates. He could care less about the 5000 pages of report he claims to have studied in preparation for his fiction book.

If you read Mercurio's quoted statement. Notice how he purposely say Roach and Harris took the victim to **whatever place** and **somewhere.** Why is he avoiding saying, Roach and Harris took her to the **railroad tracks**? It is because he knows and understand how ridiculous this would sound to logical people. Let me go a bit further and let you hear what Mercurio confesses to in this brilliant conclusion of his. I hope you're ready, because it blew my mind as well. Alright fasten your seatbelts:

"IF THE FIRST FOUR WERE NOT INVOLVED THEN:

If the first four were not involved then I would have had to _conspire_ with McHugh, whom I had never met, to frame the first four. We would have had to _invent a set of facts that we thought would match the evidence_ and tell them to repeat them.......... The polygraph would have had to be wrong on all three who took it. *The States Attorney from Felony Review and the prosecutors would have either*

been unable to discover any of these lies told by all of these people or <u>decided to conspire with everyone else</u>."

Did he say, "invent a set of facts that <u>*we*</u> thought would match the evidence...."? Truth destroys fiction any time they meet, and Peter Karl has surely met the truth in me. The States Attorney from Felony Review that Mercurio is snitching on, is Susan Sussman. Why is it so important to James Mercurio and the gang to advance the two-abduction theory? It is because the confessions contain details only the real killers and the *police* would know. If it's known that there was only one abduction by Roach and Harris, the signed confessions become the smoking-gun of one of the most diabolical and despicable acts in the history of the City and its police department. It would show that these people had no respect for Lori Roscetti, her family, the Roscetti 4 or the good people of our City, Chicago.

Well, today we know that only Roach and Harris abducted Lori and that Duane Harris admitted at the time of questioning, that he discarded her car keys after his departure from the railroad tracks. This fact is undisputed! If anyone doubt me. Go to YouTube and type in my channel **Algorithmic Power.** I will allow you to hear Duane Roach in his own words. Eddie Harris too. Smile.

Truth really need no support. Now, I will easily defend the

honorable Robert K. Ressler since he's not here to defend himself.

Today we know that the confessions are police fabrications, just like Kathleen T. Zellner, our former attorney said on the Dateline program. Knowing every detail in Marcellius Bradford's confessions was made up by Mercurio and the gang. This shows that when Marcellius was arrested on January 27, 1987 by James Mercurio and John McHugh. They *already had* in their minds, who would be the candidates for Mr.

Ressler's hijacked profile. They went to Bradford apartment knowing full well, that they were going to plant a false confession on him, including *the names* of the other boys who fit Ressler's profile. Names, already chosen by them, for destiny. All the names in Bradford's original false confession were known to these criminals before Bradford was arrested. That is, Omar Saunders, Larry Ollins, Calvin Ollins and Marcellius Bradford. Just like all the details of the crime scene, including the stick, was known to Mercurio and the gang. The 6 known false details planted in the confession reveal that all the *factual details* of the crime scene were planted by the same people who thought up the **6 known *false details*.** Robert K. Ressler was not lying, he spoke the truth. Known Liars (i.e. Mercurio and the gang) calling an honorable man a liar. The irony.

Chapter 21

The Smoking Gun

I would love to hear the great Peter Karl try and explain away the 6 known false details in the confessions of Calvin and Bradford since he publicly attributed them to the Roscetti 4. This one statement alone, undermines his fiction book, operating theory, and the two abductions that could have happen on the night of a blood moon. Good try! But Mercurio and the gang already played that card back in 2002 and were soundly put to rest, in real time. Smile.

Just because we're quiet doesn't mean we're dead. We know our place in history and we're humbled. We were given the highest form of pardons. **Pardons based upon innocence**. These pardons are not given lightly by the State of Illinois. There was no opposition from the State's Attorney to our pardons. Everyone clapped and cheered for us. Because what was understood needed no explanation. It is sad that anyone would attempt to tarnish official pardons, based upon innocence, granted from the highest office of our State. Peter Karl should really be ashamed of himself and anyone else for pushing that type of material. He even implies in his fiction book that the new investigators coerced confessions from Duane Roach. My fault it's fiction, right?

Were we all children like Calvin? Of course not. Our backgrounds reflect that the rest of us got into trouble as juveniles. That has never been a secret. In fact, it's public record. That's how Mecurio and the gang selected us, from our **backgrounds**. Smile.

However, would this be grounds or a justification to disregard the fact that these people invented a scenario, built from the profile, of an expert FBI profiler? This is the reason they settled out of court for millions of dollars. Our City was completely aware of these facts and wanted to limit the damages. So, a trial was out of the question. Today I regret I didn't take it to trial because the facts articulated in this book are not widely known. I mean, people know Roach and Harris committed this crime. But exactly how we were framed has never been investigated by the proper authorities. A conspiracy originating with the police and Felony Review. That included a host of others.

Think about it. 22 semen stains! How are you an expert Serologist and miss 20 semen stains? Pamela Ann Fish (Serologist), James Maurer, James Mecurio, Thomas Lahm, Susan Sussman (Felony Review), Patrick O' Brien and George Velcich (Prosecuting Attorneys), Thomas R. Allen (Omar's Defense Attorney), Thomas Royce (Calvin's Defense Attorney), Gregory Schlessinger (Larry's Defense Attorney), Judge

Christy S. Berkos and Marcellius Bradford's attorney all knew the blood type of the semen on the vaginal swab to be **type O secretor (i.e. Lewis positive)**. All the appointed counsels knew that the Roscetti 4 were **non-secretors (i.e. Lewis negative)**. Which meant the Roscetti 4 were not the donor of the blood type of the semen.

No one thought to say: *"Hey, wait a minute! None of these kid's blood type match the blood type of the semen recovered from Lori Roscetti. The theory is that these four raped and murdered her and the semen is from them. Something is terribly wrong here!"*

Did all these people miss this or was the conspiracy deeper than anyone could have imagined? Let's go a little deeper into my memories. Pamela Ann Fish turned over to the prosecutors and defense attorneys many laboratory reports. But I will talk about the **Laboratory Report dated October 20th, 1987!** This report made it crystal clear none of the

Roscetti 4 were Lewis positives (i.e. secretors). In fact, this report was proof that the Lewis System was one of the 11 testing systems, employed by Pamela fish to determine the secretor status of suspects in the Roscetti case. All of Defense counsel knew this because they had the report. In fact, she used the Lewis System to determine the secretor status of the seminal fluid on the vaginal swab (i.e. Exhibit K2). That's how she knew that the blood type was O secretor! The Lewis System.

In the trial of Calvin Ollins, in Judge Christy S. Berkos chamber, Pamela Ann Fish is questioned about the Lewis System, one of the 11 systems used at that time at the Chicago Police Crime Lab. When Asked by Calvin's attorney about the Lewis Enzyme System regarding Exhibit K2 (i.e. Vaginal Swab). She testified she did not conduct test under the Lewis System on the vaginal swab. During Calvin's trial she reluctantly admit that the vaginal swab contained type O secretor blood. But deny that Calvin was a non-secretor or that she found Calvin

Ollins to be a non-secretor from the saliva sample submitted to her. Although in the report dated October 20th, 1987, she clearly found Calvin Ollins, Larry Ollins, Omar Saunders and Marcellius Bradford all to be non-secretors.

Calvin was the first to go to trial and I was the second. During my trial the blood type of the vaginal swab is totally omitted. Thomas Allen knew that the O secretor blood type found on the vaginal swab didn't match me or my codefendants and never raised it during my trial. He told me that he sat in Calvin's trial. In fact, during my trial, Thomas Allen ask Pamela Ann Fish, the following closing question of his cross examination:

"*Q.   Did you do any further testing of the vaginal swab and blood workup on the four individuals?*

A.   There was no further testing for me to do on that vaginal swab so therefore I ended my testing."

I still get angry when I realize what Thomas R. Allen did to me. He never gave me this report because he understood, that I would have never allowed him to defend me the way he did. I wrote to the Attorney Registration Disciplinary Commission regarding an issue with Mr. Allen while in prison. I wish I had known that he hid this report from me. I would have pushed to have had him disbarred. I think he's a judge now. I wonder if I still can.

Chapter 22

Aiding and Abetting the conspiracy

Larry Ollins went to trial last. Me, Calvin and Larry all had separate jury trials. Prosecutors Patrick O'Brien and

George Velcich prosecuted all three trials, and Judge Christy Berkos presided over each trial, and was intricately aware of the semen evidence. At Larry's trial what Pamela Ann Fish hid during Calvin's trial was completely revealed. It blows my mind even now, when I read what was revealed in Judge Berkos' courtroom regarding what Pamela Fish new about the vaginal swab. In this trial, it was clear that Pamela Fish had committed perjury and that the prosecutors and judge knew it. Below is Larry's attorney, Gregory

Schlessinger, cross examining Pam Fish:

"Q. Could you tell the ladies and gentlemen of the jury – I don't want you to go through all of the 11 systems, but for example, could you tell them about the Lewis (phonetic spelling) system? Did you perform any tests for the classification under the Lewis system?

A. Yes, I can.

Q. Could you describe that system of classification for the ladies and gentlemen of the jury?

A. The Lewis system, although it's not considered one of the genetic markers we test for, is a system where we look for antigens from red blood cells.

What we do is, we actually take a small specimen of the blood, put it on a microscopic slide, apply commercially-prepared antiserum for the agglutination of the red blood cells, for the clumping of the red blood cells.

If the clump is in specific antisera, then they are considered to be a Lewis positive. If they do not clump, they are considered to be a Lewis negative.

Q. What is the significance of that type of classification? What does that tell you as a serologist in the crime lab?

A. We use Lewis only as a tool that would possibly aid us in determining if a person is possibly a secretor or not.

Q. Now, you mentioned the word *"secretor,"* and I would like you to try to explain, as best you can in terms that are most understandable as you can, what the term *"secretor"* means.

A. Secretor is an individual who will secrete their ABO blood group substances in bodily fluids other than blood. For example, in their semen.

Q. So, is it true that some people are secretors and some people are not secretors?

A. That's correct.

Q. And does that mean, am I correct in saying, that that means that some people can be classified in the ABO system, from **their semen**

or their saliva, because they secrete those characteristics in their other bodily fluids?

A. Some individuals you can classify that way, that is correct.

Q. And those people are called secretors, is that right?

A. That is correct.

Q. And the people that don't secrete those classifications in their saliva, or in their semen, are referred to as non-secretors, isn't that correct?

A. That's correct, for a general term, yes.

Q. Now, what does the term *"H activity"* mean?

A. H activity is basically indicative of type O blood. You cannot, when you are doing blood testing, actually see the reactions that occur with type O blood. What we actually see is, we see some interaction with a specific chemical substance, and if you see a chemical reaction, you are seeing H activity, which means you are seeing the reactions caused by type O blood.

Q. Now, if you see that H activity in a sample of either semen or saliva or in fluid other than blood, what does that indicate to you?

A. If I see -- could you repeat it, please?

Q. Yes. If you see or observe or detect, by your testing -- let me strike the question. Where could you detect H activity?

A. There are thousands of places you can detect H activity.

Q. Could you detect it in human blood?

A. Yes, sir, you can.

Q. Can you detect it in saliva?

A. Yes, sir.

Q. Could you detect it in semen in some individuals?

A. Yes.

Q. If you detect it in saliva or in semen, what does that indicate to you as a serologist in the crime laboratory?

A. If you detect it in somebody's saliva, it would indicate that somebody would be secreting that H substance.

Q. Now, they are secreting it because they are a secretor, is that correct?

A. That's correct.

Q. Now, did you make a determination as to whether Lori Roscetti was a secretor or a non-secretor?

A. Yes, I did.

Q. What was the determination that you made?

A. It was determined that Lori Roscetti was a non-secretor.

Q. *All right. And you had a vaginal specimen or vaginal swab in connection with this case, did you not?*

A. *That's correct.*

Q. And you also had a specimen from Larry Ollins, did you not?

A. That's correct.

Q. And you referred to that specimen, you had a specimen of his blood, and you had a specimen of his saliva at some point, did you not?

A. That's correct.

Q. And did you make certain observations or conclusions as to this blood and his saliva concerning his secretor status?

A. From the blood cells that I received or I tested from Larry Ollins, I determined that he was a non-secretor.

Q. All right. Just so we're clear, you determined from your testing that Lori Roscetti was a non-secretor, and you determined from your testing that Larry Ollins was a non-secretor, is that correct?

A. When I tested the blood cells from both of those individuals, I determined that they both were non-secretors.

Q. *All right. Now, you had a vaginal swab or specimen that was marked as exhibit K2 in your report, is that correct?*

A. *That's correct.*

Q. *And you made certain tests or conducted certain tests with regard to that specimen, did you not?*

A. *That's correct.*

Q. *And you noted the presence of H activity in that specimen, did you not?*

A. *That's correct.*

Q. *Now, is it not correct that someone that was a secretor deposited semen in Lori Roscetti?*

A. *That's correct.*

Remember, at my trial she was ask did she perform any other test on the vaginal swab, and her answer was no. Why didn't Judge Christy Berkos intervene? At Calvins trial in his chamber she lied and said the Lewis system was not used regarding the vaginal swab. I humbly say, the conspiracy was bigger than the police. And from the forgoing dialogue. It looks like he was a part of it! He witnessed first-hand, perjury, and the show continued.

During the closing arguments at Larry Ollins trial, Patrick O'Brien makes the following **remarkable statement** which shows what he and all the rest understood about the secretor status of the Roscetti 4:

"And just as Larry Ollins is a non secretor, could not have

accounted for the O blood type, who is O blood type but Calvin Ollins."

This single statement explains why at Calvin's trial these conspirators hid the fact, Calvin Ollins was a non-secretor as noted in the October 20th, 1987 Laboratory Report, and why none of the trial attorney raised the issue as to **our collective secretor status in regard to the O secretor blood type of exhibit K2 (i.e. Vaginal Swab).** Had the three separate Juries known, that none of us, just like Larry, were blood type **O** *secretor*. There would be no need for this book. Extraordinary efforts were made to hide exculpatory evidence that could have save four teenagers from one of the most unethical events in history. The police reports, Serologist reports and Trial transcripts are still there. I dare any of them or the family members of those who are dead and gone, to challenge the facts of this memoir. Say its libel and meet me in a courtroom. You will be soundly defeated! We are tired of the foolishness of unethical people playing with a tragedy that has scarred our family and the Roscetti family. No one will defame us, ever again. This book is written to repel them all! Truth wins. Following is the Appellate decision of the final appeal of the real killers. This appeal is not about their innocence in the rape/homicide of Lori. **They are not challenging their convictions for <u>rape</u> and <u>murder</u>.** It's about their sentences.

Chapter 23

The Killers Accept Their Fate

Appellate Court of Illinois,

First District, Sixth Division.

The PEOPLE of the State of Illinois, Plaintiff-Appellee, v. Eddie HARRIS, Defendant-Appellant.

No. 1-06-2557. Decided: July 25, 2008

In October 2003, defendant and codefendant Duane Roach were charged with 16 counts of murder in connection with the repeated rape and beating death of Lori Roscetti on October 18, 1986. On December 16, 2004, defendant and codefendant Roach each agreed to plead guilty to one count of murder (count VI), i.e., murder executed during the course of a criminal sexual assault and committed in an exceptionally brutal and heinous manner, in exchange for a 75-year extended-term sentence, 3 years of mandatory supervised release (MSR), and the dismissal of the remaining charges. Defendant was represented by Assistant Public Defender (APD) LaFonzo Palmer at the plea hearing and codefendant Roach was represented by APD Tony Eben. The trial judge specifically asked defendant if that was his "understanding of the offer," to which defendant replied, "yes."

Prior to accepting defendant's plea, the trial judge admonished him that the murder counts carried a possible sentence of 20 to 40 years with a MSR term of 3 years. The judge also admonished him that he was eligible for an extended-term sentence, whereby he could be imprisoned for up to 80 years and serve 3 years of MSR. The judge further advised defendant that he could be found eligible for the death penalty or life imprisonment on some of the charges that had been filed against him.

The trial judge advised defendant that he had "the right to continue to plead not guilty and to require the State to prove [him] guilty beyond a reasonable doubt" as well as the right to plead guilty. When asked if he understood that, defendant said, "yes." Defendant stated that he understood what a jury trial and bench trial were and that he had a right to a bench or jury trial but wished to give up those rights. Defendant then signed a jury waiver, which the trial court accepted. The judge informed defendant that by pleading guilty, he was giving up the right to confront witnesses and to call witnesses in his defense as well as the right to testify in his own defense or remain silent. The trial judge then asked the following questions of defendant.

"THE COURT: To each of you, are you pleading guilty freely and voluntarily, Mr. Harris?

DEFENDANT HARRIS: Yes.

* * *

THE COURT: Each of you have any threats, force or promises of any kind aside from the State's offer been directed against you in order to make you plead guilty, Mr. Harris?

DEFENDANT HARRIS: No."

The trial judge found that defendant understood the charges against him, the possible penalties that could be imposed, and that he was freely and voluntarily pleading guilty to murder under count VI.

The State offered the following FACTUAL BASIS:

Allen Radner would testify that in the early morning hours of October 18, 1986, at approximately 1 a.m., he walked Lori Roscetti to her car after studying late for medical school finals in the school library. David Sachs would testify that he was a railroad security officer and at approximately 4:40 a.m. on October 18, 1986, he discovered the "horribly beaten and still bleeding body" of Lori Roscetti lying next to her car on the railroad access lane located at approximately 1500 West 15th Place in Chicago.

Roscetti was pronounced dead at the scene. Joanne Richmond would testify that she was an assistant medical examiner in 1986 and she performed the autopsy on Roscetti. Roscetti was 23 years old at the time of her death and the cause of death was multiple blunt force trauma. She would testify that "virtually every bone in [Roscetti's] face was shattered, including her sinuses, her hyaloid bone, her Adam's apple[,] that [Roscetti] had been brutally stomped on, and that the medical examiner also saw the bloody shoe prints on her torso." Additionally, "there were multiple fractures of her rib cage, her torso was also torn by multiple lacerations, revealing that a sharp pointed object had been repeatedly shoved through her skin."

DNA analysts would testify that they performed numerous tests from the rape kit swabs, Roscetti's clothing, and hairs found on her clothing and in the car. These analysts would testify that "the vaginal swab was positive for Eddie Harris' DNA; the rectal swab was positive for both Harris' and Roach's DNA; that [Roscetti's] coat had seven semen stains on it belonging to [codefendant Roach]. In addition, there were semen stains on her jacket from Roach, her jogging pants from defendant and Roach including a mixture from both, her shirt from Roach and a mixture from both, her left shoe from defendant and a mixture from both, and on her underwear from Roach." Another DNA analyst would testify that three pubic hairs were recovered from the crime scene and Roscetti's clothes, two were from Roach and one was from defendant. Additionally, a fingerprint examiner would testify that partial fingerprints from the interior door of Roscetti's car were a match to defendant's fingerprints.

A police detective would testify that in January 2002, he spoke with Bernard Roach, codefendant Roach's brother. Bernard revealed that he knew the identity of Roscetti's killers and then an investigation focused on defendant and codefendant Roach.

Bernard Roach would testify that in late 1986, he was walking with his brother, codefendant Roach, and defendant near the crime scene. There were many reward posters up seeking information on Roscetti's murder. As they were walking, codefendant Roach pointed to one of the posters and said to Bernard that they did that, "Me and Eddie did that, and she was a tough bitch to kill." Bernard would further testify that "nothing else was said and that he never thought it was true until he saw the DNA exclusions and two profiles that kept coming up."

Lieutenant Joseph Murphy would testify that defendant was arrested on February 4, 2002, and he gave oral admissions and both he and codefendant Roach gave separate reenactment videos. In the reenactment video, they said they were looking for cars to break into to get money to buy crack cocaine. They came upon Roscetti, who was parked behind her building, searching for something in her car. They came up behind her, jumped her and abducted her. They drove her car to the place where she was murdered.

The State would also introduce the videotaped confessions from both defendant and codefendant Roach. The videotaped confessions would show that they abducted Roscetti and forced her into the backseat. She was held down so she could not escape or cry out. She was crying, shaking and begging to be let go. They took her to an isolated railroad access lane. They took turns raping her. Afterward, she begged to be let go and said she would give her money to them. They beat her, her face was crushed with a concrete brick or rock and her neck was repeatedly slammed in the door.

APD Palmer stipulated to these facts and that the chain of custody was maintained for all exhibits and DNA testing. The trial judge found an enough factual basis for defendant's plea and entered the judgment.

The end.

The *silver bullet* of truth does not need a lengthy dissertation to kill these types of wolves. Just enough bullets to let them know, we are no longer frighten little boys afraid of wolves with no teeth.

EPILOGUE

The Dream

It would take me years, to come into the understanding, of why I was permitted to have that dream of Lori so many years ago, and what it meant. When I think about the forces we were up against. The Goliath of lies. When I reflect upon the hatred directed at us because of those lies. When I think about the tremendous pain that we all suffered. The countless nights crying and asking God. Why? I would wonder. Was it because of the bad things I had done as a kid? I would plead with God, to give me another chance, that I would never steal or commit another burglary again.

He gave me and my friends that chance. And like the boy who cried wolf. Meaning, a delinquent kid who engaged in delinquent behavior, causing the community to turn its back on him, when he cried wolf and the wolf was really upon him. God has allowed me to be a part of a circumstance much bigger than myself, and to make me a better person. How we view things and circumstances can ill affect us, if our perception is incorrect. I had to go through this to learn how to see things the way God would see it. He saw the beautiful impression Lori would leave upon the wall of time. Like a rose that loses its petals, but the scent can never be forgotten. Lori is that. Lori was not a racist in the negative connotation. She was a racist in the positive connotation, in that she wanted to help humanity (i.e. human race). She admired all and hated none.

God sometime chooses that which will bring the most attention to problems that affect humanity. Injustice is humanity's biggest issue. Was God wise in choosing Lori for a bigger purpose? Count how many innocent people have come home from prison behind the Roscetti 4. Look at how many lives have been spared in Illinois as a result of a flawed death penalty system. A system the Governor stopped after lifting the name of the Roscetti 4 along with others. Imagine how many innocent lives have been spared.

The dream makes perfect sense. God knew Lori's fate and our fate way before we were born. We were destined to become the Roscetti 4. I know this now. And I am totally convinced of it. Why you may ask? Because God sent Lori, in that dark place to tell me. Omar! "Everything is going to be alright." But..........it will take ***time***.

Author

Omar Ameer Salahadin Muhammad

DEDICATED TO:

JESSIE MAE SAUNDERS

&

LOUIS ALLEN COSEY

Made in the USA
Lexington, KY
30 October 2019